The North American Fourth Edition

CAMBRIDGE LATIN COURSE

UNIT 4

Stage Tests

Stephanie M. Pope
Norfolk Academy, Norfolk, Virginia

Richard M. Popeck
Stuarts Draft High School and Stuarts Draft Middle School, Stuarts Draft, Virginia

CAMBRIDGE
UNIVERSITY PRESS

CAMBRIDGE
UNIVERSITY PRESS

32 Avenue of the Americas, New York, NY 10013–2473, USA

Cambridge University Press is part of the University of Cambridge.

It furthers the University's mission by disseminating knowledge in the pursuit of education, learning and research at the highest international levels of excellence.

www.cambridge.org
Information on this title: www.cambridge.org/9780521525503

© Qualifications and Curriculum Activity Enterprises Limited 1998, 2001

First published 1998
7th printing 2015

Printed in the United States of America

A catalog record for this publication is available from the British Library

ISBN 978-0-521-00505-0 paperback

Table of Contents

Preface   iv

Introduction   v – vi

Stage 35 Test   1 – 9

Stage 36 Test   10 – 19

Stage 37 Test   20 – 28

Stage 38 Test   29 – 36

Stage 39 Test   37 – 45

Stage 40 Test   46 – 53

Stage 41 Test   54 – 61

Stage 42 Test   62 – 70

Stage 43 Test   71 – 77

Stage 44 Test   78 – 84

Stage 45 Test   85 – 92

Stage 46 Test   93 – 101

Stage 47 Test   102 – 111

Stage 48 Test   112 – 119

Answers to the Stage Tests   120 – 126

Student Answer Sheet   127

Preface

This test booklet has been produced by two members of the Revision Team for the North American Fourth Edition of the *Cambridge Latin Course*: Stephanie Pope and Richard Popeck. All of the tests have been written specifically for the content of the Fourth Edition of Unit 4 which varies greatly in some Stages from the Third Edition version.

In addition to the members of the writing team, many thanks are owed to Pat Bell, Stan Farrow, Cecil Mays, and Anne Shaw, who gave specific suggestions for the tests or helped proof the final manuscript. Stan Farrow's NACCP publication, *CLC Exercise Disks,* was the source for many stories as well as some grammar and derivative exercises used in these tests. Note that the sight passage used for Stage 36 is a close variation of a Stan Farrow story found in the *Unit 4 Omnibus Workbook.* The writers could not resist the temptation of using this wonderful story in the Stage Test. Great thanks are also owed to the Latin students and faculty at the various schools who have made helpful suggestions that the writers have incorporated in this new booklet.

Stephanie M. Pope
Norfolk Academy
Norfolk, Virginia

Introduction

This booklet is designed to aid teachers who are new to the reading approach to the study of Latin, and to provide the veteran *Cambridge Latin Course* teachers with a standardized set of tests that reflect the two major objectives of the Course: "to teach comprehension of the Latin language through practice in reading it" and "to develop the students' understanding of the social and political history of the Romans, especially during the first century A.D."

Most tests start with a sight reading passage which pertains to the context of the Stage just finished. As with the textbook, a glossary is provided for the terms not covered in either the captioned line drawings that start every Stage or the *Vocabulary Checklists* that complete every Stage. Following the reading passages are comprehension and grammar questions appropriate for the content of that Stage or previous Stages. As a new feature, these comprehension/grammar questions have now been combined into one section to mirror more closely the exercises students will meet on the SAT II and the Advanced Placement exams. In some tests, selected literary passages from the Stage are carefully explored for meaning, poetic devices, and grammar constructions.

A variety of sections is provided to test the student's knowledge of grammar, derivatives, and culture. Often students are asked to prove their understanding through the manipulation of grammar points presented in the tested Stage. The grammar terms used on the tests are those actually mentioned in the textbook. Similarly, the writers have assumed that, if the meter, scansion, and poetry terms are mentioned in the textbook, then they are appropriate material for test questions. The derivative sections contain words based on the Latin words found in that Stage's *Words and Phrases Checklist* and/or *Word Study*. Culture sections are interspersed throughout the tests. Many are based upon questions found in the *Unit 4 Omnibus Workbook*.

Each test has the same format and is designed to be taken within a forty-four minute period. There are 100 machine scoreable items. For schools that do not have grading machines, a blank Student Answer Sheet is supplied so that the tests may be graded by hand. In addition, every effort has been made to standardize these tests. For instance, the headings and directions are the same for every recurring section so that students will not become confused by instructions that change with every test.

Listed below are the abbreviations used in this booklet:

abl. = ablative	indic. = indicative	plup. = pluperfect
act. = active	pass. = passive	pres. = present
imp. = imperfect	perf. = perfect	subj. = subjunctive

While these types of tests work well with many students, the writers realize that each teacher may want to emphasize different items. Teachers should feel free to adapt the tests to fit their courses or their district's requirements.

The documents in this booklet are **standardized tests** and should **never** be given to students to keep. The tests may be used by students and teachers for practice and review, but the physical test should be retained by the teachers.

Stage 35 Test

PLEASE DO NOT WRITE ON THE TEST BOOKLET.
MARK ALL ANSWERS ON THE MACHINE SCORED ANSWER SHEET.

I Directions

Read the following story.

Quintus Caecilius Iucundus cum paucis amicis in taberna loquebatur. 1
dum de sceleribus Imperatoris dicunt, aliquis Quintum rogavit num de 2
morte Paridis, pantomimi notissimi, audivisset. hac re audita, Quintus 3
scire volebat quo modo Paris mortuus esset. unus ex amicis igitur de 4
insidiis explicavit quae a Salvio, amico Imperatoris, paratae erant. 5

Quintus, fabula narrata, amicum vultu irato diu spectabat. tandem, 6
"hic vir," inquit, "nobis puniendus est. nam idem Salvius est qui regem 7
Cogidubnum in Britannia necari iussit. si eum ceperimus atque 8
puniverimus, omnes Britanni nobis gratias dabunt. itaque nobis statim 9
agendum est." 10

amicis inter se paulisper locutis, Aulus Fuscus Vulpes consilium cepit. 11
deinde summo gaudio ceteris nuntiavit: "nobis **placenta** facienda est, 12
Arcus Titi **forma**. Salvius enim, quod Haterio imperavit ut opus 13
susciperet, hoc arcu **gloriatur**. Imperator quoque, hoc arcu viso, maxima 14
admiratione affectus est. **quibus de causis** facile erit nobis Salvio 15
placentam **pro dono** offerre. placenta veneno mixta donum Salvio 16
aptissimum est." 17

quibus rebus dictis, Aulus ridebat. Quintus autem contentus non erat. 18
"quo modo," inquit, "Salvio persuadebis ut placentam ipse consumat? 19
nam Salvius, omnia suspicatus, servos habet quibus imperat ut cibum 20
ante se gustent. placentam non consumet." 21

Aulus iterum ridebat. "cum Salvio placentam dederimus, ei 22
iubebimus Salvium eam non consumere, quod donum est. Salvius 23
semper facit id quod ei non faciendum est. itaque placentam consumet!" 24

his rebus auditis, omnes amici ridebant … et culinam petebant. 25

Words and Phrases

placenta - cake
forma - shape
gloriatur: gloriari - boasts of,
    boasts about

quibus de causis - for these reasons
pro dono - as a gift
aptissimum: aptus - most suitable

II Directions

Select the answer that correctly completes the sentence.

1. **In line 1 <u>paucis amicis</u> is written in the _____ case.**
   a. nominative   b. genitive   c. dative   d. accusative   e. ablative

2. **In line 3 <u>audivisset</u> is used in an _____.**
   a. adverbial purpose clause   b. indirect command   c. indirect question

3. **In line 5 <u>paratae erant</u> is written in the _____.**
   a. perfect passive   b. pluperfect active   c. pluperfect passive

4. **In lines 1–5 the one thing we do <u>not</u> learn is that _____.**
   a. Quintus knew all about how Paris had died
   b. Salvius had prepared the plot
   c. Quintus wanted to learn how Paris had died
   d. the discussion also dealt with the crimes of the Emperor

5. **In line 6 the construction of <u>fabula narrata</u> is a(n) _____.**
   a. ablative absolute   b. active periphrastic   c. passive periphrastic

6. **In line 7 the construction of <u>puniendus est</u> is a(n) _____.**
   a. ablative absolute   b. active periphrastic   c. passive periphrastic

7. **From lines 7–8 we learn that the person who had killed Paris must be punished. We also learn that _____.**
   a. this same person had ordered Cogidubnus to be killed in Britain
   b. Quintus was very happy at the news
   c. Cogidubnus had ordered Salvius to be killed in Britain
   d. Salvius had to punish him

8. **In line 9 <u>nobis</u> is written in the _____ case.**
   a. nominative   b. genitive   c. dative   d. accusative   e. ablative

9. **In line 11 <u>locutis</u> is a _____ participle.**
   a. present active   b. perfect active   c. perfect passive

10. **From lines 12–17 we learn that _____.**
    a. Aulus wants to give Salvius a cake from the Arch of Titus
    b. Aulus wants to order Haterius to start another arch
    c. the emperor admired Salvius' boasts
    d. Aulus wants them to give Salvius a poisoned cake in the shape of the Arch of Titus

11. **In line 16 <u>Salvio</u> is written in the _____ case.**

    a. nominative   b. genitive   c. dative   d. accusative   e. ablative

12. **From lines 18–21 we learn that _____.**

    a. Quintus thinks the plan won't work

    b. Salvius has been persuaded to do what they want

    c. his slaves suspect everything

    d. Salvius orders his slaves to taste the food after he does

13. **In line 21 <u>consumet</u> is written in the _____ tense.**

    a. present   b. imperfect   c. future   d. perfect

14. **In lines 22–23 we learn that the conspirators plan to tell Salvius not to eat the cake because _____.**

    a. it is at home

    b. it is a gift

    c. he is the master

15. **In lines 23–24 Aulus claims that _____.**

    a. Salvius won't eat it

    b. Salvius always does what he is **not** supposed to do

    c. Salvius will laugh at the friends

III Directions

Select the English sentence that correctly translates the Latin sentence.

16. **audimus Glabrionem strepitu urbis vexari.**

    a. We heard that Glabrio was annoyed by the noise of the city.

    b. We hear that Glabrio is annoyed by the noise of the city.

    c. We heard that Glabrio had been annoyed by the noise of the city.

17. **scio servos cenam parare.**

    a. I know that the slaves are preparing dinner.

    b. I knew that the slaves were preparing dinner.

    c. I know that the slave is preparing dinner.

18. **Lupus dicit filium puellas et quadrigas amare.**

    a. Lupus said that his son loved a girl and a chariot.

    b. Lupus says that his son loves a girl and a chariot.

    c. Lupus says that his son loves girls and chariots.

19. **Glabrio scribit Domitianum triumphum hodie agere.**
    a. Glabrio writes that Domitian is celebrating a triumph today.
    b. Glabrio wrote that Domitian celebrated a triumph yesterday.
    c. Glabrio writes that Domitian was celebrating a triumph yesterday.

20. **putas Martialem virum quendam nimium adulari.**
    a. You thought that Martial flattered a certain man too much.
    b. You think that Martial flatters a certain man too little.
    c. You think that Martial flatters a certain man too much.

IV Directions

Select the word(s) that most closely define(s) the <u>underlined</u> *derivative.*

21. **The Gracchi promoted <u>agrarian</u> reform.**
    a. housing   b. labor   c. religious   d. land

22. **There were wells in the <u>vicinity</u>.**
    a. village   b. farm   c. area   d. oasis

23. **The museum guard behaved in an <u>officious</u> manner.**
    a. efficient   b. elderly   c. concerned   d. pompous, meddlesome

24. **The efficient busybody was <u>relegated</u> to the secretary's pool.**
    a. banished   b. suited   c. promoted   d. denied access

25. **His <u>rustic</u> manner was a clever guise.**
    a. slow-moving   c. old-fashioned
    b. out-of-practice   d. unsophisticated

26. **This sword was <u>reputed</u> to be a Civil War relic.**
    a. rejected   b. formerly believed   c. thought   d. described as

27. **The old man was an example of moral <u>rectitude</u>.**
    a. oddity   b. correctness   c. old-fashioned behavior   d. pleasure

28. **The library declared a <u>moratorium</u> on overdue fines.**
    a. period of delay   c. sincere plea
    b. doubling   d. appeal to one's sense of correctness

29. **There is one <u>caveat</u> for those interested in spelunking.**
    a. name   b. description   c. place   d. warning

30. **The students embarked on their assignments <u>simultaneously</u>.**
    a. in the same way   c. at the same time
    b. voluntarily   d. with pleasure

V   Directions

Match the Latin sentence to its English translation. One answer may be used more than once.

31. **Cicero orationes manu sua scripsit.**

32. **Cicero ad curiam orationem habitum ambulavit.**

33. **Cicero est mirabilis auditu.**

34. **Cicero in curia orationem habere potest.**

35. **Cicero ad curiam ambulavit ut orationem haberet.**

    a. Cicero walked to the senate to give a speech.
    b. Cicero wrote his speeches by means of his own hand.
    c. Cicero is able to give a speech in the senate.
    d. Cicero is amazing to hear.

VI   Directions

Match the grammar point to its Latin example.

    a. ablative of means   c. purpose clause   e. supine - accusative
    b. complementary infinitive   d. supine - ablative

36. **Cicero orationes <u>manu sua</u> scripsit.**

37. **Cicero ad curiam orationem <u>habitum</u> ambulavit.**

38. **Cicero est mirabilis <u>auditu</u>.**

39. **Cicero in curia orationem <u>habere</u> potest.**

40. **Cicero ad curiam ambulavit <u>ut orationem haberet</u>.**

VII Directions

Match the Latin definition to its character.

41. **Agricola**

42. **Britannia**

43. **Caledonii**

44. **Domitianus**

45. **Germani**

a. imperator qui triumphum falsum de Germanis celebrabat

b. populi qui a Domitiano non victi sunt

c. insula ubi Romani bellum contra Caledonios gerunt

d. populi qui ferocissimi omnium Britannorum esse creduntur

e. dux Romanus qui bellum contra Caledonios gerit

****

46. **Glabrio**

47. **Helvidius**

48. **Lupus**

49. **Martialis**

50. **Ovidius**

a. scriptor epistulae qui ruri erat

b. poeta qui versus elegantes scribit sed Imperatorem nimium adulatur

c. scriptor epistulae qui in urbe erat

d. poeta qui versus scribit qui Lupum delectabant.

e. filius scriptoris epistulae qui ruri erat

****

51. **Plinius**

52. **servi Hispaniae**

53. **Silanus**

54. **Vespasianus**

55. **Virgines Vestales**

a. populi in triumpho qui veste Germana induti sunt

b. vir qui cum Agricola in Britannia nuper militabat

c. vir dives qui nonnullas villas ruri habet

d. feminae quae incesti damnatae erant et occisae sunt

e. imperator qui patrem Lupi occidi iusserat

VIII Directions

Indicate in what type of home the following features would have been present.

    a. city townhouse   b. country villa   c. both

56. shops in front of the building

57. **triclinium**

58. long colonnades

59. complete set of baths

60. indoor plumbing

61. extensive views of the countryside

62. farmland

63. front door overlooked the street

64. **culina**

65. located on the coast or in the hills

IX Directions

Match the correct English meaning to the Latin word.

66. annosus

67. bellicosus

68. fumosus

69. verbosus

70. victoriosus

a. aggressive

b. wordy

c. old

d. successful in conquests

e. smoky

X Directions

Read the following paragraph and match the Latin word to the <u>underlined</u> English translation.

The Roman concept of <u>free time</u> meant freedom from the <u>business of life</u>, yet much of their free time was devoted to <u>learning and studying</u> which included reading and writing. Notes, short letters, and first drafts of literary works were written on <u>wax tablets</u>, while important correspondence or completed books were written on <u>pages of papyrus</u>.

71. free time

72. business of life

73. learning and studying

74. wax tablets

75. pages of papyrus

a. cerae

b. chartae

c. otium

d. negotium

e. studia

XI Directions

Select the correct answer for the following culture statements.

76. **A book, which consisted of many strips of papyrus glued together, was called a(n) _____.**
    a. amanuensis   b. notarius   c. librarius   d. volumen

77. **Select the Latin word that does NOT apply to slaves used as secretaries.**
    a. amanuensis   b. notarius   c. librarius   d. volumen

78. **Indicate the literary genre the Romans claimed to have invented.**
    a. oratory   b. didactic poetry   c. verse satire   d. pastoral poetry

79. **Indicate the second literary genre that literary critics offer as one of Rome's most distinctive literary legacies.**
    a. novel   b. comedy   c. tragedy   d. letter writing

80. **Select a trait that is not a usual characteristic of the second literary genre.**
    a. multiple themes   b. a greeting   c. a body   d. a valediction

XII Directions

Indicate the authors described by the following statements.

    a. Cicero   b. Pliny the Younger

81. He lived in the first century B.C.

82. He lived in the first and second centuries A.D.

83. He was an orator and a lawyer.

84. His letters were polished and written with an eye for publication.

85. His letters were like newsletters dealing with a variety of topics.

XIII Directions

Match the meaning to the English derivative.

86. cautious   a. one who makes a humble request

87. emeritus   b. a journeying or traveling

88. officiate   c. careful to avoid danger

89. peregrination   d. to act in a position of authority in a game, etc.

90. suppliant   e. retired from service, but retaining one's title

 Stage 35

XIV Directions

*Indicate which picture the Latin words describe. Use **a** for the picture on the left and **b** for the picture on the right.*

| a | b |

91. otium   96. flumen

92. clientes   97. quies

93. strepitus   98. umbra

94. ager   99. pompa

95. basilica   100. aves

Stage 36 Test

PLEASE DO NOT WRITE ON THE TEST BOOKLET.
MARK ALL ANSWERS ON THE MACHINE SCORED ANSWER SHEET.

I Directions

Read the following story.

poeta Martialis per urbem contendit ut amicum visitet. **libellum** novum	1
secum fert quod bene scit hunc amicum **epigrammata** audire semper	2
cupere. per forum transiens, animadvertit magnam turbam prope **rostra**	3
ridere atque clamare.	4
"puto me **propius** appropinquare debere," sibi inquit, "ut cognoscam	5
cur haec turba rideat. suspicor enim aliquid ridiculum accidere … et tu,	6
Martialis, semper rebus ridiculis delectaris!"	7
poeta, postquam propius appropinquavit, senem in rostris stantem ut	8
de libello recitet conspicatur. tamen, quotiens recitationis **initium** fecit,	9
turba magnis clamoribus **cachinnat**. tandem omnibus paulisper	10
tacentibus, senex incipit:	11
"dicis amore tui **bellas** ardere puellas,	12
qui **faciem** sine aqua, Sexte, **natantis** habes."	13
primo auditores nihil dicunt, quod haec verba intellegere non possunt.	14
"quomodo", inquit unus auditorum, "potest Sextus sine aqua natare?	15
hoc epigramma stultum est." tum auditores senem vituperare	16
deridereque incipiunt.	17
Martialis, qui nunc **irascitur**, sibi dicit,	18
"hic senex tam stultus est ut epigrammata mea auferat neque verba	19
intellegat. Sextus *sub* aqua, non *sine* aqua natat. caudex!"	20
dum Martialis haec sibi cogitat, senex aliud epigramma recitare	21
conatur:	22
"Thaida Quintus amat. 'quam Thaida?' 'Thaida **caecam**.'	23
nullum oculum Thais illa habet, ille duos."	24
Martialis, qui se **continere** iam non potest, exclamat, "satis! satis! hic	25
asinus mea epigrammata delet! amici! vos hortor ut **mihi** dicere **liceat**."	26
auditores, qui Martialem agnoscunt, tacent ut poeta seni respondeat.	27
ille, senem intente spectans, clamat,	28
"quis es, homuncule?"	29
"Fidentinus sum," inquit senex, **erubescens**.	30
"tu male recitas, amice," respondet Martialis. "sed fortasse tu melius	31
recitaris. hoc audi!	32
'quem recitas meus est, o Fidentine, libellus:	33
sed male cum recitas, incipit esse tuus.'"	34

Martiale haec verba locuto, auditores rident, plaudunt, senem e foro
agitant.

Words and Phrases

libellum: libellus - booklet

epigrammata: epigramma - epigram

rostra - the Rostra (public platform)

propius - nearer, closer

initium: initium - beginning

cachinnat: cachinnare - laugh, chortle

bellas: bellus - pretty

faciem: facies - face

natantis: natare - swim

irascitur: irasci - become angry

caecam: caecus - blind

continere - contain

mihi liceat: mihi licet - am permitted

erubescens: erubescere - blush

II Directions

Select the correct answer based on the content and the grammar of the story.

1. **In line 1 Martial was hurrying through the city to _____.**
   a. buy a book   b. see a friend   c. hear epigrams

2. **While crossing the Forum in lines 3–4, Martial _____.**
   a. noticed a big crowd near the Forum
   b. started to laugh and shout
   c. noticed a big crowd near the public platform

3. **In lines 5–7 Martial wanted to approach the commotion for every reason BUT which one?**
   a. Something ridiculous had happened.
   b. Martial was never delighted by ridiculous things.
   c. He wanted to find out what the crowd was laughing about.

4. **In line 8 <u>stantem</u> is a _____ participle.**
   a. present active   b. perfect active   c. perfect passive   d. future active

5. **When Martial arrived in lines 8–9, he saw an old man standing in order to _____.**
   a. catch sight of the book
   b. climb on the public platform
   c. recite from a book

6. **From its reaction in lines 9–10, the crowd seemed _____.**
   a. to be enjoying itself   b. to be angry   c. to be silent

7. **In lines 10–11 <u>omnibus … tacentibus</u> is an example of a(n) _____.**
   a. passive periphrastic   c. ablative absolute
   b. active periphrastic   d. ablative of means

8. **In line 14 the listeners _____.**
   a. roared with laughter
   b. howled with disbelief
   c. said nothing because they didn't understand anything

9. **In lines 18–20 Martial was amazed by how well the old man was reciting Martial's verses.**
   a. true   b. false

10. **In line 19 <u>auferat</u> is written in the _____.**
    a. present indicative   c. future indicative
    b. present subjunctive   d. imperfect subjunctive

11. **In line 20 Martial was pleased by the man's brilliant adaptation of Martial's work.**
    a. true   b. false

12. **In lines 25–26, after the man had recited a second epigram, Martial shouted that he wanted a chance to recite his own work.**
    a. true   b. false

13. **In line 27 the listeners knew Martial and quieted down to let him talk.**
    a. true   b. false

14. **In line 30 <u>erubescens</u> is a _____ participle.**
    a. present active   b. perfect active   c. perfect passive   d. future active

15. **In line 30 the old man proudly told Martial his name.**
    a. true   b. false

16. **In lines 31–32 Martial felt that the old man was better as a subject of an epigram than he was at reciting them.**
    a. true   b. false

17. **In line 32 <u>recitaris</u> is written in the _____.**
    a. present indicative   c. future indicative
    b. present subjunctive   d. imperfect subjunctive

18. **In line 32 <u>audi</u> is written in the _____.**
    a. indicative   b. subjunctive   c. imperative

19. **In line 35 <u>locuto</u> is a _____ participle.**
    a. present active   b. perfect active   c. perfect passive   d. future active

20. **In line 35 <u>auditores</u> is written in the _____ case.**
    a. nominative   b. genitive   c. dative   d. accusative   e. ablative

III Directions

Select the answer that correctly completes the following culture statements.

21. **Indicate what was NOT the usual place for a first reading.**
    a. street corner   b. patron's house   c. baths   d. barber shop

22. **The usual audience for a more comfortable first reading might include the patron, his family, and _____.**
    a. casual passers-by   c. the writer's friends
    b. slaves running errands   d. senators coming out of the **curia**

23. **The public reading of a writer's work was called a(n) _____.**
    a. recitatio   b. recitator   c. praefatio   d. auditorium

24. **The rented hall for a public reading was called a(n) _____.**
    a. recitatio   b. recitator   c. praefatio   d. auditorium

25. **The person who gave the reading was called the _____.**
    a. recitatio   b. recitator   c. praefatio   d. auditorium

26. **The introduction to the work was called the _____.**
    a. recitatio   b. recitator   c. praefatio   d. auditorium

27. **Augustus' nephew, immortalized by the poet Vergil, was _____.**
    a. Octavius   b. Marcellus   c. Caesar   d. Octavianus

28. **Public readings helped the audience _____.**
    a. enjoy a free meal
    b. decide whether or not to buy the author's work
    c. have a few hours of free entertainment

29. **The public readings were important to the author because they _____.**
    a. provided him with more examples of stories to incorporate in his next work
    b. provided him a free meal
    c. allowed him to publicize his work without the expense of publishing many copies of his book

30. **Select the description that was NOT seen at a public reading.**
    a. The writer wore a fresh toga.
    b. The writer gave an introduction.
    c. The writer stood to read his work.

IV Directions

Match the Latin word on the right to its antonym.

31. discipulus   a. accipio

32. dono   b. novus

33. plerique   c. pauci

34. vacuus   d. plenus

35. vetus   e. rhetor

V Directions

Indicate the answer to the following subjunctive statements.

36. **me rogaverunt num satis pecuniae haberem.**
    The tense of the subjunctive is _____.
    a. present   b. imperfect   c. pluperfect

37. **me rogaverunt num satis pecuniae haberem.**
    The use of the subjunctive verb is _____.
    a. indirect command   b. indirect question   c. purpose   d. result

38. **tam peritus est coquus ut ab omnibus laudetur.**
    The tense of the subjunctive is _____.
    a. present   b. imperfect   c. pluperfect

39. **tam peritus est coquus ut ab omnibus laudetur.**
    The use of the subjunctive verb is _____.
    a. indirect command   b. indirect question   c. purpose   d. result

40. **puer agricolam orat ne equum occidat.**
    The tense of the subjunctive is _____.
    a. present   b. imperfect   c. pluperfect

41. **puer agricolam orat ne equum occidat.**
    The use of the subjunctive verb is _____.
    a. indirect command   b. indirect question   c. purpose   d. result

42. **tanta erat fortitudo Britannorum ut perire potius quam cedere vellent.**
    The tense of the subjunctive is _____.
    a. present   b. imperfect   c. pluperfect

43. **tanta erat fortitudo Britannorum ut perire potius quam cedere vellent.**
    The use of the subjunctive verb is _____.
    a. indirect command   b. indirect question   c. purpose   d. result

44. **ad urbem iter facimus ut amphitheatrum a nobis visitetur.**

The tense of the subjunctive is _____.
a. present   b. imperfect   c. pluperfect

45. **ad urbem iter facimus ut amphitheatrum a nobis visitetur.**

The use of the subjunctive verb is _____.
a. indirect command   b. indirect question   c. purpose   d. result

VI Directions

Select the noun–adjective pair for each sentence.

46. **¹nox erat, et ²caelo fulgebat ³luna ⁴sereno.**
a. 1 + 2   b. 2 + 4   c. 3 + 4   d. 2 + 3

47. **¹robustus quoque iam ²tauris ³iuga solvet ⁴arator.**
a. 1 + 2   b. 2 + 3   c. 2 + 4   d. 1 + 4

48. **¹aethera contingit ²nova ³nostri ⁴principis ⁵aula.**
a. 3 + 4   b. 2 + 4   c. 2 + 3   d. 1 + 3

49. **¹aethera contingit ²nova ³nostri ⁴principis ⁵aula.**
a. 1 + 2   b. 4 + 5   c. 2 + 5   d. 2 + 3

50. **tum ¹iuvenis ²valida sustulit ³arma ⁴manu.**
a. 1 + 4   b. 2 + 4   c. 2 + 3   d. 1 + 3

VII Directions

Select the correct translation for the following sentences.

51. **nuntii dicunt hostes arma deicere.**
a. The messengers say that the enemies have thrown down their weapons.
b. The messengers said that the enemies had thrown down their weapons.
c. The messengers said that the enemies have thrown down their weapons.
d. The messengers say that the enemies are throwing down their weapons.

52. **animadverto omnes discipulos praeter te laborare.**
a. I noticed that all of the students worked besides him.
b. I notice that all of the students work besides you.
c. I notice that all of the students worked besides him.
d. I noticed that all of the students worked besides you.

53. **audimus amicos nostros multam pecuniam donare.**

   a. We hear that their friends donate no money.
   b. We heard that our friends donated no money.
   c. We hear that our friends donate much money.
   d. We heard that their friends donated no money.

54. **vicini putant agros meos vacuos esse.**

   a. The neighbors think that my fields are empty.
   b. The neighbors thought that his fields were empty.
   c. The neighbors think that their fields are empty.
   d. The neighbors thought that my fields were empty.

55. **animadvertunt Epaphroditum in auditorio adesse.**

   a. They noticed that Epaphroditus was present in the auditorium.
   b. They notice that Epaphroditus is present in the auditorium.
   c. They noticed that Epaphroditus was absent from the auditorium.
   d. They notice that Epaphroditus is absent from the auditorium.

VIII Directions

Select the Latin word(s) that correctly complete(s) the following sentences.

56. poeta notissimus est _____.   a. colloquuntur

57. in auditorio poetam exspectant _____.   b. Martialis

58. omnes inter se _____.   c. ut versus suos recitet

59. subito signum datur _____.   d. multi cives

60. auditorium intrat poeta: Martialis   e. ut taceant
    scaenam ascendit _____.

IX Directions

Select the verb written in present subjunctive.

61. a. cavebunt   b. caveant   c. cavent   d. caverunt

62. a. putetur   b. putatur   c. putabitur   d. putaretur

63. a. offendis   b. offendes   c. offendas   d. offenderes

64. a. recitatis   b. recitatur   c. recitetis   d. recitabitis

65. a. capimus   b. cepimus   c. capiemus   d. capiamus

X Directions

Select the verb written in imperfect subjunctive.

66. a. tangunt   b. tangant   c. tangent   d. tangerent

67. a. audiam   b. audirem   c. audivissem   d. audivero

68. a. respondetur   b. responditur   c. responderetur   d. respondeatur

69. a. vis   b. velis   c. volebas   d. velles

70. a. possint   b. poterant   c. possent   d. potuerunt

XI Directions

Select the correct word(s) that most closely define(s) the underlined derivative.

71. **There was difficulty in the ignition phase.**
    a. unknown   b. firing   c. compression   d. nourishing

72. **The critic animadverted the amateur presentations of "Tosca".**
    a. took notice of   c. lauded
    b. commented with disapproval on   d. was oblivious to

73. **Superman was endowed with preternatural powers.**
    a. artificial   b. imaginative   c. beyond the ordinary   d. hidden

74. **His knowledge of Roman history seemed infinite.**
    a. obvious   b. moderate   c. awesome   d. endless

75. **The story was laden with miraculous events.**
    a. ordinary   b. indescribable   c. threatening   d. marvelous

76. **The victim had a vacuous expression.**
    a. empty   b. caring   c. confused   d. intelligent

77. **He was an inveterate baseball fan.**
    a. stubborn   b. fickle   c. habitual   d. occasional

78. **The man attempted to denigrate the safety of the nuclear power plant.**
    a. criticize   b. slander   c. belittle   d. praise

79. **The parity of competition was remarkable.**
    a. equality   b. improvement   c. fairness   d. rank

80. **There is tangible evidence to support the usefulness of studying Latin.**
    a. accidental   b. slight   c. definite   d. strong

XII Directions

Match the definition to the English derivative.

81. veteran   a. empty space

82. ignite   b. one who gives

83. mirror   c. to set on fire

84. donor   d. a reflecting surface allowing one to admire oneself

85. vacuum   e. a person who has long service with an organization

****

86. tangible   a. able to bear fruit

87. tangent   b. one's equals

88. tango   c. touching but not intersecting

89. fructible   d. able to be touched

90. peers   e. a dance in which couples touch

XIII Directions

Select the correct form of the word to complete the sentence.

91. omnes (a. otium   b. otio) fruuntur.

92. ego (a. Imperatorem   b. Imperatore   c. Imperatori) non offendere conor.

93. plerique discipuli praeter (a. Marcum   b. Marco) hodie adsunt.

94. Martialis (a. Pontilianum   b. Pontiliano) iratus est.

95. Glabrio (a. Imperatorem   b. Imperatore   c. Imperatori) non miratur.

XIV Directions

Select the Latin sentence that correctly translates the English sentence.

96. **The poet knows that his words offend most listeners.**
    a. poeta scivit verba sua plures auditores offendere.
    b. poeta scit verba sua plerosque auditores offendere.

97. **I want to find out what those craftsmen are building.**
   a. cognoscere volo quid illi fabri aedificent.
   b. cognoscere volui quid hi fabri aedificarent.

98. **I would like to know why you cannot visit me.**
   a. scire volo cur te visitare non possim.
   b. scire velim cur me visitare non possis.

99. **The messengers say that the enemies are throwing down their weapons.**
   a. nuntius dicit hostes arma deicere.
   b. nuntii dicunt hostes arma deicere.

100. **We are so happy that we are singing.**
   a. tam laeti sumus ut cantemus.
   b. tam laeti eramus ut cantaremus.

Stage 37 Test

PLEASE DO NOT WRITE ON THE TEST BOOKLET.
MARK ALL ANSWERS ON THE MACHINE SCORED ANSWER SHEET.

I Directions

Read the following letter.

C. Helvidius Lupus Acilio Glabrioni amico salutem dicit.	1

amphoras vini, quas mihi misisti, libenter accepi et gratias ago. mox	2
vero gratias tibi praesenti agam; nam brevi tempore Romam reveniam.	3
ad hanc villam **ideo** veni ut ex morbo, quo affligebar, convalescerem;	4
nunc, ex morbo **recreatus**, ad urbem revenire cupio ut te ceterosque	5
amicos meos iterum videam, domum **familiam**que inspiciam, res	6
clientium administrem.	7
a **colonis** meis cotidie vexor. dicunt se totam **aestatem** diligentissime	8
laboravisse; addunt tamen se **annonam** pessimam exspectare, et me	9
orare ut auxilium sibi praebeam.	10
Helvidius, filius meus, qui nuper huc ex urbe advenit, nuntiat totum	11
populum de victoria Agricolae nunc gaudere, et in omnibus templis	12
sacerdotes victimas dis immortalibus sacrificare. cras Helvidius Romam	13
redibit; ei igitur hanc epistulam mandabo, quam tibi tradet. suspicor	14
eum ideo ad urbem quam celerrime regredi velle, ut puellam aliquam	15
visitet.	16
de te ipso, mi Glabrio, multos variosque **rumores** audio, quibus tamen	17
vix credere possum. alii dicunt te Imperatorem valde offendisse; alii	18
affirmant te in carcerem coniectum et **maiestatis** accusatum esse. nonne	19
te de ira Imperatoris saepe monui, mi amice? nisi caveris, in **iudicium**	20
sine dubio vocaberis, damnaberis, punieris. longum colloquium quam	21
celerrime tecum habere volo; nam de te valde perturbor. vale.	22

Words and Phrases

vero - indeed
ideo - for the reason
recreatus: recreare - recovered
familiam: familia - family
colonis: colonus - tenants
aestatem: aestas - summer

annonam: annona - crop
rumores: rumor - rumors
affirmant: affirmare - declare
maiestatis: maiestas - treason
iudicium: iudicium - court

II Directions

Select the correct answer based on the content and the grammar of the letter.

1. **In line 1 who is writing to whom?**
   a. Glabrio to Lupus   b. Lupus to Glabrio   c. Helvidius to Lupus

2. **In line 2 the initial purpose of the letter is _____.**
   a. to invite the reader to the country
   b. to accept an invitation to visit Rome
   c. to give thanks for a gift

3. **In line 2 misisti is written in the _____.**
   a. present active   b. perfect active   c. pluperfect active

4. **In line 3 where will the writer see his friend again?**
   a. in Rome   b. in the country   c. in a hospital

5. **In line 3 reveniam is written in the _____.**
   a. future active indicative   c. present active indicative
   b. present active subjunctive

6. **In line 4 what was the writer's original reason for coming to this place?**
   a. to visit Rome for a short while
   b. to recover from an operation
   c. to recover from an illness

7. **In line 4 convalescerem is written in the _____.**
   a. present subjunctive   b. imperfect subjunctive   c. imperfect indicative

8. **In lines 5–7 what is NOT one of the reasons the writer gives for wanting to return?**
   a. to recover from his situation
   b. to administer the affairs of his clients
   c. to see friends and family

9. **In lines 8–10 his tenants have had a great summer and expect the writer to provide help in selling their crops.**
   a. true   b. false

10. **In line 11 the writer has been visited in the city by his son.**
    a. true   b. false

11. **In lines 11–13 the son tells the news that people are happy with Agricola's victory and that the priests are sacrificing animals to the immortal gods.**
    a. true   b. false

12. **In lines 13–16 the writer says that his son will leave soon to deliver this letter to the writer's friend and to visit his girlfriend.**
    a. true   b. false

13. **In line 14 <u>redibit</u> is written in the _____.**
    a. future active indicative   c. present active indicative
    b. present active subjunctive

14. **In line 15 <u>regredi</u> is a _____ infinitive.**
    a. present active   b. present passive   c. perfect active

15. **In lines 17–18 the writer readily believes that the rumors about his friend are true.**
    a. true   b. false

16. **In lines 18–19 among the many rumors about Glabrio the two main points of view are that Glabrio has truly offended the emperor and that he is in jail charged with treason.**
    a. true   b. false

17. **In lines 20–21 the writer feels that his friend will be convicted in a court of law and punished if he is not careful.**
    a. true   b. false

18. **In line 20 <u>monui</u> is written in the _____.**
    a. present active   b. perfect active   c. future active

19. **In line 21 <u>punieris</u> is written in the _____.**
    a. pres. pass. subjunctive   b. pres. act. subjunctive   c. future pass. indic.

20. **In lines 21–22 the writer hopes to speak to his friend as soon as possible because he is upset about him.**
    a. true   b. false

III   Directions

Select the Latin sentence that correctly translates the English sentence.

21. **He is lying hidden in order to hear the old man's conversations.**
    a. latebat ut non sermonem senum audiret
    b. latet ut sermones senis audiat

22. **The originators of the example want to be seen in the senate house.**
    a. auctores exempli in curia videri volunt
    b. auctor exemplo in curiam videre voluerunt

23. **I saw the girl decorating the atrium.**

    a. puellas atrio ornantes video
    b. puellam atrium ornantem vidi

24. **The priest had led the sacrificial victim to the altar.**

    a. sacerdotes victimas ad templum duxerit
    b. sacerdos victimam ad aram duxerat

25. **The town will soon be destroyed by our army.**

    a. oppidum mox ab exercitu nostro delebitur
    b. urbs tum a copiis nostrum delebuntur

IV Directions

Select the English sentence that correctly translates the Latin sentence.

26. **scio servos cenam splendidam parare.**

    a. I know that the slave is preparing a splendid dinner.
    b. I know that the slaves have prepared a splendid dinner.
    c. I know that the slaves are preparing a splendid dinner.
    d. I know that the slave has prepared a splendid dinner.

27. **cliens putat patronum ex urbe discessisse.**

    a. The client thinks that his patron has left the city.
    b. The client thinks that his patron is leaving the city.
    c. The client thinks that the city has been left by his patron.
    d. The client thinks that the city is being left by his patron.

28. **mercator dicit templum novum in foro exstrui.**

    a. The merchant says that new temples are being built in the forum.
    b. The merchant says that a new temple is being built in the forum.
    c. The merchant says that new temples have been built in the forum.
    d. The merchant says that a new temple has been built in the forum.

29. **magister putat filium meum diligenter laborare.**

    a. The teacher thinks that her daughter is working diligently.
    b. The teacher thinks that his son has worked diligently.
    c. The teacher thinks that my daughter has worked diligently.
    d. The teacher thinks that my son is working diligently.

30. **Domitianus dicit nuntium ab Agricola missum esse.**

    a. Domitian says that the message is sent from Agricola.
    b. Domitian says that Agricola has sent a message.
    c. Domitian says that the message has been sent by Agricola.
    d. Domitian says that Agricola is sending a message.

V Directions

Select the word(s) that correctly complete(s) the sentence.

31. **ego _____ amici audire volui.**
    a. sententiae   b. sententiam   c. sententia

32. **rex _____ usus est.**
    a. huic equo   b. hunc equum   c. hoc equo

33. **cena _____ non placuit.**
    a. imperatori   b. imperatorem   c. imperatore

34. **nos _____ vidimus.**
    a. urso vulnerato   b. ursum vulneratum   c. ursi vulnerati

35. **equus _____ non credidit.**
    a. domino   b. dominum   c. domini

VI Directions

Identify the type of subjunctive use found in each sentence.

36. **Domitianus ipse adest ut fabulam spectet.**
    a. positive purpose   b. positive result   c. positive indirect command

37. **tantas divitias adeptus est ut villam splendidam iam possideat.**
    a. positive purpose   b. positive result   c. positive indirect command

38. **ducem orabimus ne captivos interficiat.**
    a. negative purpose   b. negative result   c. negative indirect command

39. **avarus timebat ne fur aurum inveniret.**
    a. negative indirect command   b. negative purpose   c. clause of fear

40. **militibus persuadeo ut marito suo parcant.**
    a. positive purpose   b. positive result   c. positive indirect command

VII Directions

*Identify the loyalty of the speakers of these passages by labeling the pro Agricola statements with an **a** and the pro Domitian statements with a **b**.*

41. Agricola credit insulam Hiberniam facile occupari posse; ego autem puto Agricolam longe errare; Hiberni enim et feroces et validi sunt.

42. tu sine causa Agricolam culpas.

43. scilicet Agricola putat se ad Britanniam missum esse ut pueros doceat, non ut barbaros superet.

44. absurdum est Agricolam revocare priusquam Britannos omnino superet!

45. quis nostrorum ducum est melior quam Agricola?

46. revocandus est Agricola et puniendus.

47. num comparas hanc inanem Agricolae victoriam cum rebus splendidis ab Imperatore nostro gestis?

VIII Directions

Indicate which officer managed the following tasks.

48. **He served abroad as an officer of a legion.**
    a. consul b. tribunus plebis c. aedile d. tribunus militum e. praetor

49. **He ran the law courts.**
    a. consul b. tribunus plebis c. aedile d. tribunus militum e. praetor

50. **He helped advise the common man.**
    a. consul b. tribunus plebis c. aedile d. tribunus militum e. praetor

51. **He managed public money.**
    a. consul   b. vigintivir   c. quaestor   d. praetor   e. aedile

52. **He managed the prisons and minting of coins.**
    a. consul   b. vigintivir   c. quaestor   d. praetor   e. aedile

53. **He managed the upkeep of the baths, sewers, and road building.**
    a. consul   b. vigintivir   c. quaestor   d. praetor   e. aedile

54. **He presided over the senate and supervised all government business.**
    a. consul   b. vigintivir   c. quaestor   d. praetor   e. aedile

IX Directions

Match the definition to the Latin term.

55. amici

56. consilium

57. cursus honorum

58. sententia

59. suo anno

a. in one's year

b. close associates of the emperor

c. opinion

d. council

e. series of offices

X Directions

Indicate whether the following culture statements are true or false by marking **a** *for* **true** *and* **b** *for* **false**.

60. Most citizens could expect to move through these career steps in the same timely fashion as other citizens and gain access to the top office.

61. The public voted on who would be members of the Emperor's Council.

62. The council included people from the senatorial and equestrian classes of society.

63. When emperors changed, all former members of the councils were immediately dropped.

64. All emperors followed the advice of their councils without any hesitation or pause for thought.

65. All council members felt that they could express their opinions with no threat of punishment from the emperor.

66. The most common task of the **amici** was to advise the emperor on matters of law.

67. Unfortunately during Domitian's reign, **amici** used their position to increase their power.

68. During Domitian's reign, **amici** used their position to spread rumors about their enemies.

69. The **cursus honorum** afforded the emperor the opportunity to learn about people's special skills.

70. Agricola was recognized for his financial acumen while Pliny the Younger gained recognition for his battle strategies.

XI Directions

Match the English derivative to its Latin root.

71. amplius   a. culpable

72. aurum   b. amplify

73. coniunx   c. indignant

74. culpo   d. conjugal

75. dignus   e. auric

****

76. incensus   a. exert

77. exemplum   b. frankincense

78. exercitus   c. dainty

79. discere   d. sample

80. dignus   e. disciplinarian

XII Directions

Identify the tense and voice of the following <u>underlined</u> infinitives.

81. **iussisti Caledonios quoque in populi Romani potestatem <u>redigi</u>.**
    a. present active   b. present passive   c. perfect active   d. perfect passive

82. **nunc tibi nuntio exercitum Romanum magnam victoriam <u>retulisse</u>.**
    a. present active   b. present passive   c. perfect active   d. perfect passive

83. **credo hanc insulam legione una obtineri <u>posse</u>.**
    a. present active   b. present passive   c. perfect active   d. perfect passive

84. **difficile est <u>intellegere</u> quale responsum Domitianus cupiat.**
    a. present active   b. present passive   c. perfect active   d. perfect passive

85. **scilicet Agricola putat se ad Britanniam <u>missum esse</u> ut pueros doceat.**
    a. present active   b. present passive   c. perfect active   d. perfect passive

XIII Directions

Match the meaning to the English derivative.

86. diva   a. giving offense

87. auriferous   b. a leading woman singer in an opera

88. invidious   c. bearing gold

89. oblivious   d. hateful; disgusting; offensive

90. odious   e. forgetful; unmindful

****

91. estivate   a. to bring into practice

92. culpable   b. cannot be excited; impassive

93. expatriate   c. blameworthy

94. imperturbable   d. to exile

95. initiate   e. to spend the summer in a dormant condition

****

96. irrevocable   a. unquestionable; cannot be doubted

97. fiat   b. lacking sense or meaning

98. indubitable   c. to deprive of legal force

99. inane   d. cannot be recalled

100. invalidate   e. an order issued by a legal authority

Stage 38 Test

PLEASE DO NOT WRITE ON THE TEST BOOKLET.
MARK ALL ANSWERS ON THE MACHINE SCORED ANSWER SHEET.

I   Directions

Read the following story.

Polla patri Clementi de marito Sparso querebatur. Clemens, quod sciebat filiam		1
Sparso invitam nupsisse, de hac re loqui nolebat.		2

Polla:	nescio, pater, cur me isti seni nubere iusseris. scio tamen eum	3
	in villa nostra per noctem numquam manere. scio quoque eum	4
	cum aliis feminis saepe visum esse. scio denique me **propter**	5
	haec ab amicis derideri. credo me Sparsum … aut me ipsam …	6
	necaturam esse, nisi …	7
Clemens:	tace! periculosum est **adfini** Imperatoris queri.	8

Clemens Pollae de nuptiis infelicibus explicare conabatur.	9

Clemens:	quamquam valde perturbaris, mea Polla, ego ipse multa	10
	odiosa facere cogor, ne Imperator Domitianus familiam meam	11
	puniat. nonne consentis etiam vitam miserrimam meliorem	12
	esse quam vitam nullam?	13
Polla:	pater, ignavissimus es! mortem quam vitam miserrimam	14
	malo. num oblitus es Helvidium, quem valde amavi, periisse,	15
	ab hoc Imperatore occisum? te oportet intellegere me quoque	16
	mortem non timere.	17
Clemens:	cur istum iuvenem commemoras? Helvidius sane stultissimus,	18
	non fortissimus, fuit … sicut **avus** eius, qui, quamquam	19
	senator notissimus erat, Imperatorem Vespasianum vituperare	20
	ausus, poenam morte suo dedit … et sicut pater, qui, quod	21
	fabulas in theatro edit, quae familiam imperatoris deridere	22
	videntur, Domitianum maxime offendit. intellegere non	23
	possum cur tu hanc gentem laudes.	24
Polla:	gentem Helvidii laudo, quod illi fortiter perire sciunt. sine	25
	dubio tu, sicut frater tuus, **ignominiose** peribis. qui, consul	26
	electus, odio Domitiano factus est, quod praeco verbo	27
	'Imperator' **pro** 'consul' **forte usus est**. tali Imperatori	28
	assentari non modo ignavum sed etiam inutile est.	29
Clemens:	et cum tali Imperatore dissentire quoque inutile est.	30
	Domitianus ipse maritum tuum elegit. si tu Sparsum … aut te	31
	ipsam … occideris, patrem tuum, et matrem, propter iram	32
	Imperatoris quoque interficies. tibi eligendum est …	33

II   Directions

Select the correct answer based on the content and the grammar of the story.

1. **In line 1 we see that Polla is _____.**
   a. questioning her father about her husband Sparsus
   b. extolling the joys of married life to her father
   c. complaining to her father about her husband

2. **In lines 1–2 the best translation for** *quod sciebat filiam Sparso invitam nupsisse* **is _____.**
   a. because he knows that his daughter married an unwilling Sparsus
   b. because he knew that his daughter had married Sparsus unwillingly
   c. because he knew that Sparsus had married his daughter unwillingly

3. **In line 2 nupsisse is a _____ infinitive.**
   a. present passive   b. perfect active   c. perfect passive

4. **In line 3 the tense and mood of iusseris is _____.**
   a. perfect subjunctive   b. future perfect indicative   c. pluperfect indicative

5. **In lines 3–6 indicate the one thing Polla does NOT know about her marriage:**
   a. Sparsus never stays home the entire night.
   b. Sparsus is often seen with other women.
   c. Sparsus is made fun of by his friends because of these things.

6. **In lines 6–7 indicate the one action Polla does NOT believe:**
   a. that she will kill Sparsus.
   b. that Sparsus will kill her.
   c. that she will kill herself.

7. **In line 8 the case of adfini is _____.**
   a. nominative   b. genitive   c. dative   d. accusative   e. ablative

8. **In line 8 the form of queri is _____.**
   a. present active infinitive   c. perfect active indicative
   b. present passive infinitive   d. perfect passive indicative

9. **In lines 9–12 Clemens is trying to _____.**
   a. promise that a divorce will happen soon
   b. explain that he, too, has to do difficult things to keep his family safe
   c. get her to agree that no life is better than a very miserable one

10. **In line 10 the tense and voice of <u>perturbaris</u> are _____.**
   a. present active   c. imperfect active
   b. present passive   d. imperfect passive

11. **In lines 14–15 from Polla's reactions we learn that she _____.**
   a. completely agrees with him
   b. would rather die
   c. would rather live a very miserable life

12. **In lines 15–17 we gather that _____.**
   a. Polla still loves Helvidius
   b. Polla doesn't understand why her father is afraid to die
   c. Polla is reminding her father that Helvidius had killed the emperor

13. **In lines 18–24 indicate the one fact we do NOT learn about Helvidius or his family.**
   a. Helvidius was very brave and very foolish.
   b. Helvidius' grandfather had cursed the Emperor Vespasian.
   c. Helvidius' father produced plays that seemed to mock the emperor's family.

14. **In lines 18–20 indicate the number of <u>different</u> verb tenses represented.**
   a. 1   b. 2   c. 3

15. **In lines 25–29 indicate the one statement that Polla actually says:**
   a. The family of Helvidius knows how to die bravely.
   b. Her father will kill his father disgracefully.
   c. It is always useful to flatter the emperor.

16. **In line 27 the case of <u>odio</u> is _____.**
   a. nominative   b. genitive   c. dative   d. accusative   e. ablative

17. **In line 27 the case of <u>praeco</u> is _____.**
   a. nominative   b. genitive   c. dative   d. accusative   e. ablative

18. **In line 27 the case of <u>verbo</u> is _____.**
   a. nominative   b. genitive   c. dative   d. accusative   e. ablative

19. **In lines 30–33 Clemens states that if Polla does what she claims, she will _____.**
   a. be killed by Sparsus
   b. be killed by the emperor
   c. cause the death of her mother and father

20. **In line 33 the form of <u>eligendum est</u> is _____ .**
    a. perfect passive indicative
    b. present active indicative
    c. gerundive of obligation

III Directions

Written below is a list of wedding customs. Indicate whether the custom was found in ancient times, only in modern situations or in both cultures by using **a** *for* **old,** **b** *for* **new,** *or* **c** *for* **both.**

21. engagement

22. sacrifice

23. marriage certificate

24. witnesses at marriage

25. wedding cake

26. ring on the 3rd finger of the left hand

27. father giving away the bride during ceremony

28. wedding feast hosted by bride's family

29. pulling bride away from mother with force

30. removal of **bulla**

31. saying traditional marriage words

32. anointing doorposts with oil

33. bride wears wedding veil

34. throwing rice / rose petals

35. parting bride's hair with a spear point

36. bride and groom are the first dance pair at the reception

37. torch-lit procession to the groom's house

38. noisy greetings and coarse jokes to groom by his friends

39. carrying the bride over the threshold

40. bride feeding first slice of cake to the groom

IV Directions

Indicate by using **a** *for* **true** *and* **b** *for* **false** *whether a Roman woman could do the following activities.*

41. vote in elections

42. was not restricted to home

43. sit on a jury

44. go to the theater

45. manage the household

46. plead in a court of law

47. go to the baths

48. take an active role in politics

49. visit friends

50. accompany husband to parties

V Directions

Match the definitions to their culture terms.

51.	sine manu	a.	marriage where bride passes to husband's control
52.	dos	b.	wedding vow
53.	flammeum	c.	bridal veil
54.	cum manu	d.	marriage where bride remains a member of father's family
55.	"ubi tu Gaius, ego Gaia"	e.	payment by bride's family to husband

****

56.	confarreatio	a.	bride undressers
57.	far	b.	engagement
58.	iunctio dextrarum	c.	ancient ceremony of eating cake
59.	matronae univirae	d.	joining of hands in marriage
60.	sponsalia	e.	sacred grain

VI Directions

Select the correct translation for these indirect statements.

61. **scio puellam a puero portari.**
    a. I know that the girl carries the boy.
    b. I know that the girl is carried by the boy.
    c. I know that the girls are carried by the boys.
    d. I know that the girl has been carried by the boy.

62. **scio puerum puellam portavisse.**
    a. I know that the boy carries the girl.
    b. I know that the boy will carry the girl.
    c. I know that the boy has been carried by the girl.
    d. I know that the boy has carried the girl.

63. **scio puerum puellam portare.**
    a. I know that the girl carries the boy.
    b. I know that the boy carries the girl.
    c. I know that the boy will carry the girl.
    d. I know that the boy has carried the girl.

64. **scio puerum puellam portaturum esse.**
    a. I know that the boy will carry the girl.
    b. I know that the boys will carry the girl.
    c. I know that the boy has carried the girl.
    d. I know that the girl has carried the boy.

65. **scio puerum a puella portatum esse.**
    a. I know that the girl is carried by the boy.
    b. I know that the boy has been carried by the girl.
    c. I know that the girl has been carried by the boy.
    d. I know that the girls are carried by the boys.

VII Directions

Read the following story. Select the correct explanation for the <u>underlined</u> words or phrases.

Julia had finally reached the [66]<u>proper age</u> for marriage but did not want [67]<u>to follow what Roman custom said she had to</u>. Her wealthy father liked 35 year-old Marcus, a member of the emperor's household, but she knew a wedding of this type would follow the [68]<u>more formal wedding ceremony</u> and the [69]<u>restrictions of this type of marriage</u> frightened her. Her love was Publius, a young noble of the [70]<u>proper age</u>, who favored the [71]<u>less restrictive marriage</u> with its [72]<u>own customs</u>. Julia knew what [73]<u>she had to do in this situation</u>, but she did not like it. While she agreed with the [74]<u>chief purpose of marriage</u>, she also believed in marrying for love, and Marcus wanted the marriage only for the [75]<u>benefits</u> he could obtain. He could care less about children or Julia.

Julia vowed to do her best in this situation and to keep a diary which she hoped would be published one day to serve as a guide for other girls caught in this unpleasant situation.

66. a. 20–21   b. 17–18   c. 15–16   d. 13–14

67. a. groom was selected at birth
    b. soothsayer foretold of the marriage
    c. father selected the groom
    d. groom was one who paid the highest dowry

68. a. cum manu   b. sine manu   c. sponsalia   d. iunctio dextrarum

69. The woman had:
    a. no house
    b. no right of divorce or dowry recovery
    c. right of divorce and dowry recovery
    d. right of selecting her own husband

70. a. 13–14   b. 15–16   c. 17–18   d. 19–20s

71. a. cum manu   b. sine manu   c. sponsalia   d. iunctio dextrarum

72. The woman had:
   - a. no house
   - b. no right of divorce or dowry recovery
   - c. right of divorce and dowry recovery
   - d. right of selecting her own husband

73. a. elope   c. follow father's orders
   b. rebel against her father   d. plead to the emperor

74. a. to pool political power   c. to pool financial resources
   b. to have children   d. to please parents

75. a. right to all his wife's property   c. right to be in the senate
   b. right to be on the emperor's **consilium**   d. right to live on the Esquiline

VIII Directions

Match the definitions to the people they describe.

76. Domitianus   a. girl forced to marry against her will

77. Domitian & Vespasian   b. new names of sons of emperor's relative

78. Flavia   c. the rich old man

79. Polla   d. current emperor

80. Sparsus   e. wife of man who lost his brother by order of the emperor

****

81. Calpurnia   a. the brother who was killed by order of the emperor

82. Clemens   b. young lover – son of Lupus

83. Helvidius   c. emperor's relative who had three children

84. Quintilian   d. third wife of a famous writer

85. Sabinus   e. famous teacher of the time

IX Directions

Match the meaning to the English derivative.

86. aptitude   a. assurance

87. rectitude   b. appearance of being real

88. gratitude   c. strict honesty

89. verisimilitude   d. a natural tendency

90. certitude   e. thankfulness

****

91. querulous   a. a person lacking knowledge

92. demented   b. having skill in using one's hands

93. ignoramus   c. mentally ill

94. dexterous   d. complaining; peevish

95. unctuous   e. oily to the touch

X Directions

Match the English derivative to its Latin root.

96. iungere   a. clandestine

97. lex   b. preliminary

98. clam   c. subjunctive

99. limen   d. ascertain

100. certus   e. illegitimate

      Stage 38

Stage 39 Test

PLEASE DO NOT WRITE ON THE TEST BOOKLET.
MARK ALL ANSWERS ON THE MACHINE SCORED ANSWER SHEET.

I Directions

Read the following story.

Titus Publiusque, filii Clementis, **versus** quosdam poetae **Ovidii**		1
legunt, quos rhetori Quintiliano postridie recitent. Titus, quod scit		2
rhetorem rogaturum esse ut primus recitet, fratri queritur:		3

Titus:	nonne putas, mi Publi, hunc Quintilianum esse hominem	4
	stultissimum? cur ego primus recitare semper cogor? cur	5
	tu secundus rogaris?	6
Publius:	credo rhetorem hoc semper fecisse, quod tu, **maior natu**,	7
	melius recitas. animadverto quoque te, orationibus	8
	perfectis, saepius quam me laudari.	9
Titus:	consilium ergo habeo! cras rogabimur ut hos versus	10
	recitemus. Quintilianus non rogabit num rem totam	11
	didicerimus. si ego primam carminis partem paravero, tu	12
	secundam, rhetor numquam intelleget se falsum esse!	13
Publius:	mihi placet!	14

postridie pueri, ad aulam regressi, a Quintiliano salutantur: 15

Quintilianus:	salvete, Tite Publique! heri versus quosdam poetae Ovidii	16
	discere conabamini. spero vos hoc carmen hodie recitare	17
	posse. sed primum velim hanc fabulam verbis vestris	18
	atque **oratione soluta** audire. Tite, incipe!	19

Titus begins to recite Ovid's tale of Pyramus and Thisbe about two star-crossed lovers who went against their parents' wishes and met at a secret place only to die by the end of their adventure.

Titus loqui desinit, quod credit rhetorem Publium rogaturum esse ut 20
ceteros versus narret. Quintilianus tamen Tito signum dat ut orationem 21
renovet. ille, quod versus ceteros fratri mandavit, nescit quid dicat. 22
celeriter tamen consilium capit, et Quintiliano explicat: 23

Titus:	domine, hanc fabulam renovare non possum. quotiens de	24
	Pyramo Thisbeque narro, de Polla, sorore nostra, et	25
	Helvidio, amato eius, puto. rem difficilem …	26

Quintilianus, qui de amore Pollae morteque Helvidii intellegit, his verbis 27
fallitur. postea tamen Titus Publiusque omnes versus discunt! 28

II Directions

Select the correct answer based on the content and the grammar of the story.

1. **In lines 1–2 we see that Titus and Publius are _____.**
   a. reading verses of Ovid that they will recite to their teacher today
   b. reading verses of Ovid that they will recite to their teacher tomorrow
   c. writing verses like Ovid's that they will recite tomorrow

2. **In lines 2–3 we find out that _____.**
   a. Titus is excited about the prospect
   b. Titus wants his brother to go first
   c. Titus is complaining because he will be asked to recite first

3. **In line 3 recitet is used in a(n) _____.**
   a. indirect command   b. indirect question   c. positive purpose clause

4. **In line 3 rogaturum esse is a _____ infinitive.**
   a. present active   b. perfect passive   c. future active

5. **In lines 4–6 we see that Titus is upset because _____.**
   a. Quintilian always asks them to recite in the same order
   b. Quintilian is a very stupid man
   c. Quintilian never does the same thing twice

6. **In lines 8–9 the best translation for the rest of this sentence is: once the recitations are finished, I notice also that _____.**
   a. you often praise me
   b. I am praised more often than you
   c. you are praised more often than I

7. **In line 7 fecisse is a _____ infinitive.**
   a. present active   b. perfect active   c. future active

8. **In lines 8–9 orationibus perfectis is used as a(n) _____.**
   a. time when   b. place where   c. ablative absolute

9. **In line 9 saepius is a _____.**
   a. positive adverb   b. comparative adjective   c. comparative adverb

10. **In line 9 laudari is a _____ infinitive.**
    a. present active   b. present passive   c. perfect passive

11. **In line 11 recitemus is used as a _____ subjunctive.**

 a. positive indirect command   b. positive purpose   c. positive result

12. **In line 12 the form of didicerimus is _____.**

 a. future perfect indicative   b. pluperfect indicative   c. perfect subjunctive

13. **In line 12 the form of paravero is _____.**

 a. future perfect indicative   b. pluperfect indicative   c. perfect subjunctive

14. **In lines 10–13 Titus devises a plan whereby _____.**

 a. he learns the second half of the poem and Publius the first half

 b. he learns the first half of the poem and Publius the second half

 c. he will never have to recite

15. **In line 19 the form of incipe is _____.**

 a. singular vocative   b. positive imperative   c. ablative singular

16. **In line 22 we learn that _____.**

 a. Publius recites his part as planned

 b. Titus finishes the speech

 c. Titus cannot continue

17. **In lines 24–26 Titus defends his actions by _____.**

 a. comparing Pyramus and Thisbe to Polla and Helvidius

 b. saying that Pyramus and Thisbe's story is not as interesting as Polla's and Helvidius'

18. **In line 27 the case of his verbis is _____.**

 a. nominative   b. genitive   c. dative   d. accusative   e. ablative

19. **In line 28 the tense, voice, and mood of fallitur are _____.**

 a. present active indicative   c. present active subjunctive

 b. present passive indicative   d. present passive subjunctive

20. **In line 28 we learn that _____.**

 a. the boys try this ploy often later on

 b. the boys teach the verses to the teacher

 c. the boys learn all of the verses thereafter

III   Directions

Indicate whether the following culture statements are true or false by marking **a** *for* **true** *and* **b** *for* **false**.

21. Writing literature was an easy way to make a fortune in ancient Rome.

22. There were no copyright laws in ancient Rome.

23. Most Roman literature was aimed at the general public.

24. Quintilian was a very famous educator in the time of Augustus.

25. All profits from book sales went to the authors.

26. Roman literature was meant to be read silently.

IV Directions

Select the answer closest in meaning to the <u>underlined</u> word.

27. **We saw no <u>fallacy</u> in the explanation.**
    a. exaggeration   b. uncertainty   c. false idea   d. promise

28. **In that situation, there is no <u>discrimination</u> between rich and poor.**
    a. prejudice   b. dividing line   c. contest   d. agreement

29. **She began her third <u>semester</u> of studies.**
    a. six-month period   b. half moon   c. four months   d. four years

30. **The city supported the establishment of an <u>arboretum</u>.**
    a. wooded park   c. wildlife refuge
    b. horticultural display   d. area for outdoor concerts

V Directions

Select the correct form of the Latin for the <u>underlined</u> English translations.

31. **audio filios Clementis a Quintiliano cotidie _____.**
    I hear that the sons of Clemens <u>are taught</u> daily by Quintilian.
    a. **docentur**   b. **docere**   c. **doceri**   d. **docuisse**

32. **cives convenient ut poetam _____.**
    The citizens will meet <u>to hear</u> the poet.
    a. **audiunt**   b. **audimus**   c. **audiant**   d. **audire**

33. **_____ ad forum a multis servis.**
    <u>I shall be carried</u> to the forum by many slaves.
    a. **portor**   b. **portabo**   c. **portaberis**   d. **portabor**

34. **vos non _____ sum.**
    I am not <u>going to punish</u> you.
    a. **puniendus**   b. **punitus**   c. **puniturus**   d. **punivisse**

35. **nobis ergo tempus est cognoscere quid _____.**
    Therefore it is time for us to find out what <u>you have learned</u>.
    a. **didiceritis**   b. **didicissetis**   c. **discatis**   d. **didicistis**

VI Directions

Indicate the use of each gerundive found in the sentences below.

a. adjective   b. purpose construction   c. obligation

36. nobis villa aedificanda est.

37. cives in theatrum fabulae spectandae gratia conveniebant.

38. femina artem librorum scribendorum discere conabatur.

39. servus aquam flammarum exstinguendarum causa quaerebat.

40. puer libros legendos amavit.

VII Directions

Select the correct English translation for each sentence.

41. poeta scit verba sua plerosque auditores offendisse.

42. poeta scit plerosque auditores a verbis suis offensos esse.

43. poeta scit verba sua plerosque auditores offendere.

44. poeta scit verba sua plerosque auditores offensura esse.

45. poeta scit plerosque auditores a verbis suis offendi.

a. The poet knows that his words offend most listeners.
b. The poet knows that his words will offend most listeners.
c. The poet knows that his words have offended most listeners.
d. The poet knows that most listeners are offended by his words.
e. The poet knows that most listeners have been offended by his words.

VIII Directions

Match the definitions to the culture items.

46. Argiletum   a. famous patron

47. Maecenas   b. Roman comic playwright

48. *Ars Amatoria*   c. book by Quintilian

49. *The Education of an Orator*   d. poem by Ovid

50. Plautus   e. booksellers' street

IX Directions

Select the type of the subjunctive clause found in each sentence.

51. **cognoscere volo quid illi fabri aedificent.**
    a. indirect command   b. indirect question   c. positive purpose

52. **senatores conveniunt ut orationem audiant.**
    a. indirect command   b. indirect question   c. positive purpose

53. **tam saevus est dominus ut servos punire numquam desinat.**
    a. positive purpose   b. result   c. indirect command

54. **ducem orabimus ne captivos interficiat.**
    a. indirect command   b. indirect question   c. positive purpose

55. **avarus timebat ne fur aurum inveniret.**
    a. indirect command   b. clause of fear   c. negative purpose

X Directions

Indicate the grammar points requested.

56. Select the adjectives from the following sentence.
    at ¹puer ²infelix ³mediis clamabat in ⁴undis.
    a. 1 + 2   b. 2 + 3   c. 3 + 4   d. 1 + 4

57. Select the nouns from the following sentence.
    at ¹puer ²infelix ³mediis clamabat in ⁴undis.
    a. 1 + 2   b. 2 + 3   c. 3 + 4   d. 1 + 4

58. Select the adjectives from the following sentence.
    reddebant ¹nomen ²concava ³saxa ⁴meum.
    a. 1 + 2   b. 1 + 3   c. 2 + 3   d. 2 + 4

59. Select the nouns from the following sentence.
    reddebant ¹nomen ²concava ³saxa ⁴meum.
    a. 1 + 2   b. 1 + 3   c. 2 + 3   d. 2 + 4

60. Select the adjectives from the following sentence.
    nunc ¹mare per ²longum ³mea cogitat ire ⁴puella.
    a. 1 + 2   b. 2 + 3   c. 3 + 4   d. 1 + 4

61. Select the nouns from the following sentence.
    nunc ¹mare per ²longum ³mea cogitat ire ⁴puella.
    a. 1 + 2   b. 2 + 3   c. 3 + 4   d. 1 + 4

62. Select the adjectives from the following sentence.
    ¹maioresque cadunt ²altis de ³montibus ⁴umbrae.
    a. 1 + 2   b. 2 + 3   c. 3 + 4   d. 1 + 4

63. Select the nouns from the following sentence.
    ¹maioresque cadunt ²altis de ³montibus ⁴umbrae.
    a. 1 + 2   b. 2 + 3   c. 3 + 4   d. 1 + 4

64. Select the adjectives from the following sentence.
    atque ¹opere in ²medio ³laetus cantabat ⁴arator.
    a. 1 + 2   b. 2 + 3   c. 3 + 4   d. 1 + 4

65. Select the nouns from the following sentence.
    atque ¹opere in ²medio ³laetus cantabat ⁴arator.
    a. 1 + 2   b. 2 + 3   c. 3 + 4   d. 1 + 4

XI Directions

Indicate whether the following statements are true or false by marking **a** *for* **true** *and* **b** *for* **false**.

66. Quintilian was an educator and a lawyer.

67. Quintilian was the first teacher to obtain a salary from the state.

68. Quintilian was paid by Vespasian to teach poetry.

69. Quintilian taught Pliny the Younger.

70. Quintilian wrote in his book that some of Ovid's work was excellent.

XII Directions

Indicate the author described by the following statements.

   a. Cicero   b. Ovid   c. Martial   d. Pliny the Younger   e. Vergil

71. His banker friend had a slave make copies of his work.

72. He was a wealthy writer.

73. He was helped and encouraged by Maecenas and Augustus.

74. He wrote a love manual and had a scandal with the emperor's family.

75. He often wrote flattering remarks about the emperor to stay out of trouble.

XIII Directions

Indicate whether the following statements apply to **a** *modern literature or to* **b** *ancient literature.*

76. It is written to be read aloud.

77. Authors can earn a living at writing.

78. It is written to be read silently.

79. There are strict copyright laws.

80. The content is aimed at all types of audiences.

81. It is read to the public to increase sales.

82. The authors receive extensive training in public speaking.

83. It is written for a more dramatic effect and with a more artistic word order.

84. Just as with a score of music, it must be read aloud to achieve the full effect.

85. It is heavily influenced by the rhetorical nature of the author's education.

XIV Directions

Select the correct form of the verb to complete the sentence.

86. **Glabrio timebat ne Imperator ab eo graviter _____.**
    a. offendisset   b. offensus esset

87. **nisi orationem diligenter audiveritis, verbis blandis _____.**
    a. falletis   b. fallemini

88. **fessus sum! cotidie centurio me laborare _____.**
    a. iubet   b. iubetur

89. **medicus te sanavit, ubi morbo gravi _____.**
    a. afficiebas   b. afficiebaris

90. **tu semper bene recitas; semper rhetor te _____.**
    a. laudat   b. laudatur

XV Directions

Match the meaning to the English derivative.

91. intersperse
92. dissimulate
93. perdition
94. decadence
95. capillary

a. to hide by pretense
b. complete and irreparable loss
c. a tiny blood vessel
d. deterioration; decay
e. to scatter among things

****

96. campus
97. sporadic
98. coincidence
99. transliterate
100. soprano

a. the highest female voice
b. an accidental occurrence of events at the same time
c. to write in the characters of another alphabet
d. occasional
e. the grounds of a college

Stage 40 Test

PLEASE DO NOT WRITE ON THE TEST BOOKLET.
MARK ALL ANSWERS ON THE MACHINE SCORED ANSWER SHEET.

I   Directions

Read the following story.

Gaius Salvius Liberalis, cum intellexisset se in exilium mitti, filium   1
paucosque amicos qui eum adiuverant arcessivit ad gratias eis agendas.   2
filio prope eum stante, affirmavit se favorem eorum numquam   3
obliturum esse.   4

   "nos amicitia auxilioque vestro valde movemur. si veremini ne   5
princeps vos quoque puniat, hortor ut me in exilium sequamini."   6

   Haterius, cliens Salvii, processit ad se cum patrono iungendum.   7

   postridie Haterius, villam Salvii ingressus, patronum librum legentem   8
invenit. qui, Haterio ingresso, tristis respexit atque, librum tollens, haec   9
verba amico fideli dixit: 10

   "ecce poeta Ovidius, ab imperatore suo in exilium quoque damnatus.   11
audi **versus** eius: 12

        'alloquor extremum *maestos* abiturus *amicos*   13
            qui modo de multis unus et alter erat.   14
        uxor amans flentem *flens* acrius *ipsa* tenebat,   15
            imbre per **indignas** usque *cadente* **genas**.   16
        nata procul **Libycis** aberat *diversa* sub **oris**   17
            nec poterat *fati* certior esse *mei*.'"   18

   Salvius, his verbis recitatis, librum in lectum deposuit atque lacrimis   19
se dedit.   20

Words and Phrases

versus: versus - verses
alloquor: alloqui - speak to, address
extremum - for the last time
maestos: maestus - sad
modo - just now, recently

de multis - reduced from many
unus et alter - one or two
flentem: flere - weep
acrius - more bitterly
imbre: imber - rain, showers, tears

Notes to assist with the poem

In each line, adjective–noun units are marked with italics, or (where there are two units in one line) with bold type as well.

line 13: **abiturus** describes the subject of **alloquor**

line 14: **multis** and **unus et alter** both refer to the word which **maestos** describes

line 15: **flentem** describes **me** (understood), the writer of the poem

indignas: indignus - guiltless	diversa: diversus - remote, distant
usque - continually	oris: ora - shore, land
genas: gena - cheek	fati: fatum - fate, fortune
nata - daughter	certior esse - be informed (of)
Libycis: Libycus - Libyan, African	

II   Directions

Select the correct answer based on the content and the grammar of the story.

1. **In lines 1–2 Salvius summoned his son and a few friends when _____.**
   a. he was in exile
   b. he had returned from exile
   c. he had realized he was going into exile

2. **In line 1 the tense and mood of <u>intellexisset</u> are _____.**
   a. imperfect indicative   c. pluperfect indicative
   b. imperfect subjunctive   d. pluperfect subjunctive

3. **In line 1 the form of <u>mitti</u> is _____.**
   a. present active infinitive   c. perfect passive infinitive
   b. present passive infinitive   d. future active infinitive

4. **In line 2 the friends who were with Salvius _____.**
   a. had helped Salvius
   b. had given thanks to Salvius for his help
   c. had summoned him to their homes

5. **In line 2 the tense and mood of <u>adiuverant</u> are _____.**
   a. imperfect indicative   c. pluperfect indicative
   b. imperfect subjunctive   d. pluperfect subjunctive

6. **In line 2 the use of <u>agendas</u> is _____.**
   a. adjective   b. purpose construction   c. ablative absolute

7. **In lines 3–4 Salvius had wanted to thank his friends and to tell them that he would _____.**
   a. forget them forever
   b. never forget their favor
   c. forget their favor

8. **In line 3 <u>stante</u> is a _____ participle.**
   a. present active   b. perfect active   c. perfect passive

9. **In line 4 the form of <u>obliturum esse</u> is _____.**
   a. present active infinitive
   c. perfect passive infinitive
   b. present passive infinitive
   d. future active infinitive

10. **In lines 5–6 Salvius suggested that his friends _____.**
   a. move with him because of friendship and by means of his help
   b. not fear the emperor
   c. go with him if they feared the emperor

11. **In line 5 the tense, voice, and mood of <u>movemur</u> are _____.**
   a. present active indicative
   c. present passive indicative
   b. present active subjunctive
   d. present passive subjunctive

12. **In line 6 the tense, voice, and mood of <u>puniat</u> are _____.**
   a. present active indicative
   c. present passive indicative
   b. present active subjunctive
   d. present passive subjunctive

13. **In line 6 the tense, voice, and mood of <u>sequamini</u> are _____.**
   a. present active indicative
   c. present passive indicative
   b. present active subjunctive
   d. present passive subjunctive

14. **In line 7 Haterius came to _____.**
   a. become Salvius' patron
   b. join himself with a new patron
   c. join himself with his patron Salvius

15. **In lines 8–9 the next day Haterius found Salvius _____.**
   a. reading a book
   b. entering the house
   c. looking for a new patron

16. **In line 8 <u>ingressus</u> is a _____ participle.**
   a. present active   b. perfect active   c. perfect passive

17. **In line 8 <u>legentem</u> is a _____ participle.**
   a. present active   b. perfect active   c. perfect passive

18. **In line 8 the use of <u>legentem</u> is _____.**
   a. adjective   b. purpose construction   c. ablative absolute

19. **In line 9 the use of <u>ingresso</u> is _____.**
   a. adjective   b. purpose construction   c. ablative absolute

20. **In line 11 Salvius and Ovid had this in common:**
   a. that they were both exiled by emperors.
   b. that they both wrote poetry.
   c. that they were exiled by the same emperor.

21. **In line 11 damnatus is a _____ participle.**
    a. present active   b. perfect active   c. perfect passive

22. **In line 12 the form of audi is _____.**
    a. vocative   b. adverb   c. imperative   d. perfect passive participle

23. **In lines 13–14 in his poem Ovid addresses _____.**
    a. many friends
    b. a few friends
    c. his wife and daughter

24. **In line 15 Ovid and his wife are _____.**
    a. crying together
    b. falling because of the rain
    c. informing their daughter together

25. **In lines 19–20 when Salvius had finished the reading, he _____.**
    a. picked up the book
    b. cried to the book
    c. began to weep

III Directions

Select the correct translation for the following indirect statements.

26. audio discipulum librum legere.
27. audio discipulum librum legisse.
28. audio discipulum librum lecturum esse.
29. audivi discipulum librum legere.
30. audivi discipulum librum legisse.

a. I hear that the student will read the book.

b. I hear that the student is reading the book.

c. I hear that the student has read the book.

d. I heard that the student had read the book.

e. I heard that the student read the book.

****

31. audivi discipulum librum lecturum esse.
32. audio librum a discipulo legi.
33. audio librum a discipulo lectum esse.
34. audivi librum a discipulo legi.
35. audivi librum a discipulo lectum esse.

a. I hear that the book is read by the student.

b. I heard that the book has been read by the student.

c. I heard that the book had been read by the student.

d. I heard that the student would read the book.

e. I hear that the book has been read by the student.

IV Directions

Match the kind of court or judge in Roman times to the crime.

36. inheritance cases

37. murder

38. senatorial crimes

39. civil (non-criminal)

40. criminal offenses

41. legacy

42. treason

43. property damage awards

44. adultery

a. **quaestiones**

b. **praetor**

c. court of **centumviri**

d. court of **senatores**

V Directions

Select the best translation for the following indirect statements.

45. **audivi tres Virgines Vestales damnatas esse.**
   a. I hear that three Vestal Virgins are being condemned.
   b. I heard that three Vestal Virgins were condemned.
   c. I hear that three Vestal Virgins have been condemned.
   d. I heard that three Vestal Virgins had been condemned.

46. **puto poetam optime recitare.**
   a. I thought that the poet recited very well.
   b. I think that the poet will recite very well.
   c. I think that the poet recites very well.
   d. I thought that the poet would recite very well.

47. **servus credit multos Romanos invitari.**
   a. The slave believes that many Romans are invited.
   b. The slave believes that many Romans were invited.
   c. The slave believed that many Romans have been invited.
   d. The slave believed that many Romans had been invited.

48. **sentio milites fidem servaturos esse.**
   a. I felt that the soldiers would keep their word.
   b. I feel that the soldiers will keep their word.
   c. I felt that the soldiers had kept their word.
   d. I feel that the soldiers are keeping their word.

49. **speravimus ducem auxilium mox missurum esse.**
    a. We hope that the general will soon send help.
    b. We hope that the general has already sent help.
    c. We hoped that the general would soon send help.
    d. We hoped that the general had already sent help.

50. **Glabrio scit Salvium Domitianum offendisse.**
    a. Glabrio knew that Salvius offended Domitian.
    b. Glabrio knows that Salvius has offended Domitian.
    c. Glabrio knows that Salvius offends Domitian.
    d. Glabrio knew that Salvius had offended Domitian.

VI Directions

Indicate whether the following culture statements are true or false by marking **a** *for* **true** *and* **b** *for* **false**.

51. In Roman times there were state prosecutors.

52. In Roman times there were no police.

53. In Roman times a criminal was tried by a public official.

54. In Roman times a government department handled all prosecutions.

55. All Romans were prosecuted by private individuals.

VII Directions

Match the definition to its character.

56. Agricola
    a. imperator in hac fabula

57. C. Salvius Liberalis
    b. dux Romanus in Britannia

58. Cogidubnus
    c. uxor revocata imperatoris

59. Domitia
    d. rex in Britannia

60. Domitianus
    e. senator qui damnatus est

****

61. L. Marcius Memor	a. pumilio qui de Domitia Parideque narravit
62. M. Acilius Glabrio	b. heros noster
63. Myropnous	c. amor mortuus uxoris imperatoris
64. Paris	d. senator Romanus qui imperatorem non amat
65. Q. Caecilius Iucundus	e. haruspex in Aquis Sulis qui contra Salvium testimonium dedit

****

66. Q. Haterius Latronianus	a. domus nova effigiei Salvii
67. Rufilla	b. filius Salvii
68. Tiber Flumen	c. iudex in cognitione
69. L. Ursus Servianus	d. uxor Salvii
70. Vitellianus	e. amicus fidelis et cliens Salvii

VIII Directions

*Indicate whether the following sentences contain either **a** gerund or **b** gerundive.*

71. nobis villa aedificanda est.

72. cives in theatrum spectandae causa conveniebant.

73. femina artem scribendi discere conabatur.

74. servus aquam flammarum exstinguendarum causa quaerebat.

75. puer legendum amavit.

IX Directions

Match the definition to the culture term.

76. decemviri legibus scribendis	a. unknown politician
77. duodecim tabulae	b. ten-man board established to write laws
78. iudex	c. first set of laws from 450 B.C.
79. leges	d. individual judge
80. novus homo	e. laws

X   Directions

Match the Latin word to its antonym.

81. benignus   a. angustus

82. durus   b. levis

83. fidelis   c. malignus

84. gravis   d. mollis

85. latus   e. perfidus

XI   Directions

Match the meaning to the English derivative.

86. alleviate   a. to combine; to join

87. associate   b. depraved; unprincipled

88. mutate   c. office where a foreign diplomat resides

89. consulate   d. to lighten or relieve

90. reprobate   e. to change

****

91. infamy   a. noisy and violent

92. configuration   b. rosy; ruddy

93. utensil   c. disgrace; dishonor

94. florid   d. a kitchen implement

95. tumultuous   e. an arrangement of parts

XII   Directions

Match the English derivative to its Latin root.

96. obicere   a. infamous

97. crimen   b. feign

98. fama   c. premeditation

99. meditari   d. objection

100. fingere   e. recriminate

Stage 41 Test

PLEASE DO NOT WRITE ON THE TEST BOOKLET.
MARK ALL ANSWERS ON THE MACHINE SCORED ANSWER SHEET.

I   Directions

Read the following letter.

difficile est, domine, exprimere verbis quantam **perceperim laetitiam**,	1
quod et mihi et **socrui** meae praestitisti ut **adfinem** eius Caelium	2
Clementem in hanc provinciam transferres. ex illo enim **mensuram**	3
beneficii tui **penitus** intellego, cum tam plenam indulgentiam cum tota	4
domo mea **experiar**, cui referre gratiam parem ne audeo quidem. itaque	5
ad **vota confugio** deosque precor ut eis quae in me **adsidue confers** non	6
indignus existimer.	7

Words and Phrases

perceperim: percipere - take hold of
laetitiam: laetitia - happiness
socrui: socrus - mother-in-law
adfinem: adfinis - relative
mensuram: mensura - measure
penitus - inwardly

experiar: experiri - experience
vota: votum - vows
confugio: confugere - have recourse to
adsidue - continuously
confers: conferre - bestow, grant
indignus - unworthy

II   Directions

Select the correct answer based on the content and the grammar of the letter.

1. **In line 1 Pliny is having trouble expressing _____.**
   a. how disappointed he is
   b. how happy he is
   c. how sad he is

2. **In line 1 the tense and mood of <u>perceperim</u> are _____.**
   a. pluperfect indicative   c. perfect subjunctive
   b. future perfect indicative

3. **In line 2 the case of <u>socrui</u> is _____.**
   a. nominative   b. genitive   c. dative   d. accusative   e. ablative

4. **In lines 2–3 Trajan has transferred to Bithynia _____.**
   a. Pliny's mother-in-law's relative
   b. Pliny's relative
   c. the emperor's relative

5. **In line 3 the tense and mood of <u>transferres</u> are _____.**
   a. present indicative   b. future indicative   c. imperfect subjunctive

6. **In lines 3–5 Pliny understands the full extent of the Emperor's indulgence now that it _____.**
   a. affects the empire
   b. affects Pliny's whole family
   c. affects only Pliny

7. **In line 4 the translation of the first <u>cum</u> is _____.**
   a. with   b. when   c. although

8. **In line 4 the translation of the second <u>cum</u> is _____.**
   a. with   b. when   c. although

9. **In line 5 <u>cui</u> refers to _____.**
   a. the emperor   b. the deed   c. Pliny's mother-in-law

10. **In line 5 Pliny _____.**
    a. wants to pay the emperor back equally
    b. cannot hear the thanks
    c. will not dare pay him back equally

11. **In line 6 Pliny will _____.**
    a. confuse the vows and pray to the gods
    b. keep the vows and pray to the gods
    c. flee from the job

12. **In line 6 <u>vota</u> is written in the _____ case.**
    a. nominative   b. genitive   c. dative   d. accusative   e. ablative

13. **In lines 6–7 Pliny wants _____.**
    a. to be considered worthy of the emperor's gifts
    b. to be rated continually as unworthy
    c. to confer unworthy gifts on himself

14. **In line 6 <u>eis</u> is written in the _____ case.**
    a. nominative   b. genitive   c. dative   d. accusative   e. ablative

15. **In line 7 <u>existimer</u> is written in the _____.**
    a. present passive indicative
    b. future passive indicative
    c. present passive subjunctive

III Directions

Indicate the speakers of these lines.

   a. Pliny the Younger   b. Ulpian   c. Vergil

16. There is nothing more civilized than stable government and nothing more precious than liberty.

17. Remember that you rule people by your government.

18. The governor of a province has greater powers in that province than anybody except the emperor.

19. An honest and conscientious governor ought to see that the province he governs is peaceful and undisturbed.

20. Bear in mind that you are being sent to the province of Achaea, the very heart of Greece, … "to set in order the affairs of the free cities."

IV Directions

Select the correct Latin word to complete the following sentences.

21. **nescio quatenus Christiani puniri** (a. **solent** b. **soleant**).

22. **nescio utrum venia paenitentiae** (a. **datur** b. **detur**) **necne**.

23. **nescio utrum nomen ipsum, sine flagitiis, an flagitia sola** (a. **puniantur** b. **puniuntur**).

24. **interrogavi ipsos utrum Christiani** (a. **erant** b. **essent**) **necne**.

V Directions

After selecting the correct form of the verb for the sentences listed above, match these general statements to the Latin sentences to which they apply.

   a. I conducted the questioning myself.
   b. Should I be lenient if the prisoner shows a change of heart?
   c. Just how much should I punish a Christian?
   d. Do I punish ones called Christians without evidence or do I punish just the ones with evidence?

25. **nescio quatenus Christiani puniri** (**solent/soleant**).

26. **nescio utrum venia paenitentiae** (**datur/detur**) **necne**.

27. **nescio utrum nomen ipsum, sine flagitiis, an flagitia sola** (**puniantur/ puniuntur**).

28. **interrogavi ipsos utrum Christiani** (**erant/essent**) **necne**.

VI Directions

Select the correct translations for the conditional sentences.

29. **si laborabo, laetus ero.**
    a. If I work, I am happy.
    b. If I work, I will be happy.
    c. If I would work, I would be happy.

30. **nisi laboravero, non laetus ero.**
    a. If I work, I am happy.
    b. If I work, I will be happy.
    c. If I do not work, I will not be happy.

31. **si laboro, laetus sum.**
    a. If I work, I am happy.
    b. If I work, I will be happy.
    c. If I do not work, I will not be happy.

VII Directions

*Select the correct translation for the word **cum** in the following sentences.*

   a. when   b. since   c. although

32. <u>cum</u> magistra nostra aegra sit, magistram novam hodie habemus.

33. <u>cum</u> librum legissem, rem statim intellexi.

34. <u>cum</u> librum non vidisset, rem tamen intellexit.

35. <u>cum</u> nos de periculo monuissetis, aliquid quam celerrime fecimus.

VIII Directions

*Indicate whether the following culture statements are true or false by marking **a** for **true** and **b** for **false**.*

36. It is unusual that we have a large number of details about the day-to-day operation of provincial rule in Bithynia under Pliny's rule.

37. The Emperor Trajan appointed Pliny the governor of Bithynia.

38. The provincial governor at this time is usually selected by the emperor.

39. Under Emperor Domitian the Roman Empire reached its largest expanse.

40. The emperor could appoint a governor instead of leaving the choice to the senate.

41. Pontius Pilate was one of the best-known proconsuls.

42. No one except for the emperor had more power in the Roman provinces than the Roman governors.

43. Saint Peter appealed his arrest in Judea.

44. Pliny was instructed to investigate the financing and construction of public buildings in his province.

45. The Bithynians were known for their careful spending of funds for public projects.

IX Directions

Match the definitions to the correct culture terms.

46.	Bithynia	a.	became part of the empire by Roman invasion.
47.	Britain	b.	was a province with an equestrian governor.
48.	Dacia	c.	was the first Roman territory gained.
49.	Judea	d.	became part of the empire by bequest.
50.	Sicily	e.	was the last Roman territory gained.

****

51.	iuridicus	a.	title of the governor of an imperial province
52.	legatus Augusti	b.	title of the governor of a senatorial province
53.	legiones/auxilia	c.	title of the equestrian provincial governors
54.	praefecti	d.	governor's troops to protect the province
55.	proconsul	e.	Roman who took charge in the law courts while the governor of a province carried on with fighting

X Directions

Select the correct response to answer the culture questions or to complete the culture statements.

56. **What was NOT a governor's duty?**
    a. to protect the province against attack from the outside
    b. to protect the province against rebellion from inside
    c. to administer the law in his province by traveling around acting as a judge
    d. to post soldiers in jobs normally done by civilians

57. **What was NOT an accepted use of the governor's soldiers?**
    a. to conquer further territory for the province
    b. to guard prisons
    c. to deal with problems such as bandits or pirates
    d. to serve as officials on the governor's staff

58. **Agricola was sent to Britain because of his _____.**
    a. work as a military tribune and as a legionary commander
    b. work in two treasury offices
    c. work with building architects

59. **Pliny the Younger was sent to Bithynia because of his _____.**
    a. work as a military tribune and as a legionary commander
    b. work in two treasury offices
    c. work with building architects

60. **By Trajan's time there was an improvement in the treatment of provinces as evidenced in Trajan's replies that showed his concern for the people who were known as _____.**
    a. mandata   b. publicanus   c. prospectus

61. **The provincial tax collector was called the _____.**
    a. mandata   b. publicanus   c. prospectus

62. **The instructions given to provincial governors by the emperor were called _____.**
    a. mandata   b. publicanus   c. prospectus

XI Directions

*Indicate whether the following statements written by Tacitus refer to **a** the Britons under Agricola or to **b** the Romans as seen by the Scots.*

63. They plunder the whole world.

64. Individuals and communities are encouraged to build temples, forums, and houses.

65. The people referred to colonnades, baths, and elegant dinner parties as "civilization."

66. They not only devastate the land but scour the sea.

67. They describe robbery and slaughter as "empire."

68. Education is provided for the sons of chieftains.

69. They turn lands into deserts and call it "peace."

70. They often use Latin to make speeches.

XII Directions

*Indicate whether the following statements about taxation in the provinces are true or false by marking **a** for **true** and **b** for **false**.*

71. In the first century B.C. Roman governors were feared and hated for their greed and cruelty.

72. Tax collection was contracted out to the highest bidders.

73. The highest bidder was required to make up any deficit to what his contract called for.

74. The tax collectors often gave refunds to the provincial citizens if they collected too many taxes.

75. The tax collectors demanded high taxes to make profits for themselves.

XIII Directions

Indicate the subjunctive uses found in the following sentences.

76. **rogo ut scribas mox.**
    a. indirect question   b. indirect command   c. positive purpose

77. **incertus sum utrum carcerem custodire debeam per publicos servos an per milites.**
    a. indirect question   b. indirect command   c. positive purpose

78. **recte vereris ne utrique neglegentiores sint.**
    a. negative purpose   b. indirect command   c. clause of fearing

79. **in principiis manebas ut de modo poenae consulereris.**
    a. positive result   b. indirect command   c. positive purpose

80. **cognovi quot servi punirentur.**
    a. negative purpose   b. indirect question   c. relative purpose

XIV Directions

*Indicate the writer of the following passages by using **a** for **Trajan** and **b** for **Pliny**.*

81. nihil opus est … ad continendas custodias plures commilitones converti.

82. Sempronius Caelianus, egregius iuvenis, repertos inter tirones duos servos misit ad me …

83. sicut saluberrimam navigationem usque Ephesum expertus …

84. tibi quidem secundum exempla complurium in mentem venit posse collegium fabrorum apud Nicomedenses constitui.

85. usque in hoc tempus … neque cuiquam diplomata commodavi neque in rem ullam nisi tuam misi.

86. refert autem voluntarii se obtulerint an lecti sint vel etiam vicarii dati.

87. rogo … utrum per publicos civitatum servos … an per milites adservare custodias debeam.

88. nec dubitandum fuisset, si exspectasses donec me consuleres, an iter uxoris tuae diplomatibus, quae officio tuo dedi, adiuvandum esset, cum apud amitam suam uxor tua deberet etiam celeritate gratiam adventus sui augere.

89. nam et tu dabis operam ut manifestum sit illis electum te esse, qui ad eosdem mei loco mittereris.

90. dispice an instituendum putes collegium fabrorum dumtaxat hominum CL.

XV Directions

Match the meaning to the English derivative.

91.	benignity	a.	variety
92.	diversity	b.	a truth
93.	incendiary	c.	devotion to religious duties
94.	piety	d.	a kind act
95.	verity	e.	capable of causing fire

XVI Directions

Match the English derivative to its Latin root.

96.	consuetudo	a.	exculpate
97.	culpa	b.	institutionalize
98.	instituere	c.	accustom
99.	merere	d.	precept
100.	praecipere	e.	meretricious

Stage 42 Test

PLEASE DO NOT WRITE ON THE TEST BOOKLET.
MARK ALL ANSWERS ON THE MACHINE SCORED ANSWER SHEET.

I Directions

Read the following story.

adversus omnes fortis veloces **feras** canis cum domino semper **fecisset**	1
satis, languere coepit annis **ingravantibus**. aliquando obiectus hispidi	2
pugnae **suis arripuit** aurem: sed **cariosis** dentibus **praedam** dimisit. hic	3
tunc venator dolens canem **obiurgabat**. cui senex contra **Lacon**: "non te	4
destituit animus, sed **vires** meae. quod fuimus, lauda, si iam damnas,	5
quod sumus."	6

Words and Phrases

adversus - against
feras: fera - wild beasts
fecisset satis: satisfacere - to satisfy
languere - to be weak
ingravantibus: ingravare - weigh down
aliquando - after some time
obiectus: obicere - to throw before, to expose
hispidi: hispidus - bristly, hairy

suis: sus, suis - boar
arripuit: arripere - seize at
cariosis: cariosus - decayed
praedam: praeda - prey, booty
obiurgabat: obiurgare - scold
Lacon - Laconian (hound)
vires: vis - strength

II Directions

Select the correct answer based on the content and the grammar of the story.

1. **How was the dog described?**
   a. brave   b. swift   c. wild   d. satisfying to his master

2. **What kind of dog was he?**
   a. hunting   b. herding   c. lap dog   d. house

3. **What started affecting the dog?**
   a. blindness   b. lameness   c. old age   d. hoarseness

4. **What did the dog try to grab?**
   a. a foot   b. an ear   c. a piece of gold   d. a hank of hair

5. **What is the case of <u>dentibus</u>?**
   a. nominative   b. genitive   c. dative   d. accusative   e. ablative

6. **What gave out on the dog?**
   a. his sight   b. his legs   c. his bark   d. his teeth

7. **What is the form of <u>dolens</u>?**
   a. present active participle   c. perfect passive participle
   b. perfect active participle   d. future active participle

8. **What is a synonym for <u>obiurgabat</u>?**
   a. verberabat   b. laudabat   c. vituperabat   d. curabat

9. **What is the case of <u>cui</u>?**
   a. nominative   b. genitive   c. dative   d. accusative   e. ablative

10. **What has deserted the dog?**
    a. his courage   b. his men   c. his strength   d. his sight

11. **What is the mood of <u>lauda</u>?**
    a. indicative   b. imperative   c. subjunctive   d. infinitive

12. **What is the tense of <u>fuimus</u>?**
    a. present   b. imperfect   c. future   d. perfect   e. pluperfect

13. **What does the dog suggest his master do?**
    a. accept him the way he is
    b. praise what he is
    c. condemn what he is
    d. condemn what he was

14. **What is the tense of <u>sumus</u>?**
    a. present   b. imperfect   c. future   d. perfect   e. pluperfect

III Directions

Indicate the grammar points requested.

15. Select the adjectives from the following sentence.
    ¹multas per ²gentes et ³multa per ⁴aequora vectus
    a. 1 + 2   b. 1 + 3   c. 2 + 3   d. 2 + 4

16. Select the nouns from the following sentence.
    ¹multas per ²gentes et ³multa per ⁴aequora vectus
    a. 1 + 2   b. 1 + 3   c. 2 + 3   d. 2 + 4

17. Select the adjectives from the following sentence.
    ¹ferreus ²assiduo consumitur ³anulus ⁴usu
    a. 1 + 2   b. 1 + 3   c. 2 + 3   d. 2 + 4

18. Select the nouns from the following sentence.
    ¹ferreus ²assiduo consumitur ³anulus ⁴usu
    a. 1 + 2   b. 1 + 3   c. 2 + 3   d. 3 + 4

19. Select the adjectives from the following sentence.

tres adeo ¹incertos ²caeca ³caligine ⁴soles
a. 1 + 2   b. 1 + 3   c. 2 + 3   d. 3 + 4

20. Select the nouns from the following sentence.

tres adeo ¹incertos ²caeca ³caligine ⁴soles
a. 1 + 2   b. 1 + 3   c. 2 + 3   d. 3 + 4

IV Directions

Read the following poem by Catullus.

cenabis bene, mi Fabulle, apud me	1
paucis, si tibi **di** favent, diebus,	2
si tecum **attuleris** bonam atque magnam	3
cenam, non sine **candida** puella	4
et vino et **sale** et omnibus cachinnis.	5
haec si, **inquam**, attuleris, **venuste** noster,	6
cenabis bene ...	7

Words and Phrases

di: deus - god
attuleris: afferre - bring
candida: candidus - fair complexion

sale: sal - salt, wit
inquam - I say
venuste: venustus - charming

V Directions

Select the correct answer based on the content and the grammar of the poem.

21. **To what is the poet inviting Fabullus?**
a. funeral   b. wedding   c. dinner

22. **The celebration _____.**
a. is happening now
b. happened a few days ago
c. will happen in a few days

23. **Who must grant permission to Fabullus?**
a. the host   b. the gods   c. the days

24. **What is the tense of <u>cenabis</u>?**
a. present   b. imperfect   c. future   d. perfect

25. **What is the case of <u>diebus</u>?**
a. nominative   b. genitive   c. dative   d. accusative   e. ablative

26. **What modifies <u>diebus</u>?**

    a. cenabis   b. mi   c. paucis

27. **What will make the event a success?**

    a. if Fabullus pays for the meal
    b. if Fabullus brings the food and entertainment
    c. if Fabullus makes a sacrifice to the gods

28. **What is the tense of <u>favent</u>?**

    a. present   b. imperfect   c. future   d. perfect

29. **What is the tense of <u>attuleris</u>?**

    a. present   b. imperfect   c. future   d. future perfect

30. **How do you translate <u>attuleris</u>?**

    a. you bring   c. you have brought
    b. you will bring   d. you had brought

31. **What is NOT something else Fabullus should bring?**

    a. a girl   b. wine   c. jokes   d. money

VI Directions

Match the definition to the correct poetry term.

32. allusion

33. connotation

34. figurative language

35. parallelism

36. sound effects

    a. language that departs from the literal standard meaning in order to achieve a special effect
    b. the use of certain combinations of letters to express a feeling or mood
    c. brief reference to details the writer expects the reader to recognize
    d. the cluster of implicit or associated meanings of a word as distinguished from that word's specific meaning
    e. recurrence or repetition of a grammatical pattern

****

37. chiasmus

38. imagery

39. interlocked word order

40. juxtaposition

    a. words of one noun–adjective phrase alternating with those of another (ABAB)
    b. a criss-cross arrangement of words (ABBA)
    c. two words or phrases set side-by-side to intensify the meaning
    d. the use of vivid language to represent objects, action, or ideas

VII Directions

Match the person to a characteristic or a work.

   a. Horace   b. Quintilian   c. Pompeian citizen

41. *Ars Poetica*

42. Wrote from the perspective of a rhetorician

43. Wrote from the perspective of a poet

44. "I wonder, o wall, that you have not collapsed with the boring weight of so many writers."

45. *Institutio Oratoria*

VIII Directions

*Indicate whether the following poetry statements are true or false by marking **a** for **true** and **b** for **false**.*

46. Latin poetry is based on rhythm, i.e. the pattern of long and short vowels in a line.

47. English poetry is based on natural word accents to give it rhythm.

48. Relying on Greek antecedents, pronunciation of Roman syllables was similar to reading music with each syllable representing musical time.

49. Roman poetry is filled with abundant use of rhetorical devices.

50. Since Latin is an inflected language, the poet may arrange the words in an order to create pictures not only by meaning but by placement.

51. Successful interpretation of Roman poetry requires the reader to have a clear understanding of classical mythology, history, and geography.

IX Directions

*Select the translation that is **NOT** correct.*

52. **ecce! deus fio.**
   a. Look! I am being made into a god.
   b. Look! I am making a god.
   c. Look! I am becoming a god.

53. **nihil in culina fiebat.**

   a. He was doing nothing in the kitchen.
   b. Nothing was happening in the kitchen.
   c. Nothing was being done in the kitchen.

54. **res ridicula facta erat.**

   a. A silly thing had been done.
   b. A silly thing had happened.
   c. He had done a silly thing.

55. **ignorabamus quid in curia fieret.**

   a. We were unaware of what he was doing in the senate.
   b. We were unaware of what was happening in the senate.
   c. We were unaware of what was being done in the senate.

X   Directions

Select the word(s) that best express(es) the meanings of these English derivatives.

56. **mollify**   a. soothe   b. weigh   c. criminalize

57. **lugubrious**   a. light   b. mournful   c. portable

58. **memento**   a. moment of time   b. souvenir   c. christening

59. **cecum**   a. surrender   b. season   c. blind intestinal pouch

60. **sidereal** – deals with   a. earth   b. moon   c. stars

XI   Directions

Match the author to the clue that describes him.

   a. Catullus   b. Horace   c. Ovid   d. Phaedrus   e. Vergil

61. His chief work was the *Aeneid*.

62. He was a **libertus Augusti** and wrote many fables.

63. Born the son of a freedman auctioneer, this poet was an immediate literary success in Rome.

64. He was a talented poet who died at an early age and who wrote a touching tribute to his brother.

65. He was a facetious poet who wrote a guide for young lovers.

XII Directions

Select the theme that best describes each of the following passages.

Themes
- a. There has to be a morning after.
- b. Live for today.
- c. It is easier to bear hard things by accepting them.
- d. Parting is such sweet sorrow.
- e. The just don't always prevail.

66. carpe diem, quam minimum credula postero.

67. "ante hos sex menses male" ait "dixisti mihi."
respondit agnus: "equidem natus non eram."
"pater hercle tuus" ille inquit "male dixit mihi;"
atque ita correptum lacerat, iniusta nece.

68. nunc tamen interea haec, prisco quae more parentum
    tradita sunt tristi munere ad inferias,
accipe fraterno multum manantia fletu,
    atque in perpetuum, frater, ave atque vale.

69. tempore difficiles veniunt ad aratra iuvenci,
    tempore lenta pati frena docentur equi.

70. ipse diem noctemque negat discernere caelo
nec meminisse viae media Palinurus in unda.
tres adeo incertos caeca caligine soles
erramus pelago, totidem sine sidere noctes.
quarto terra die primum se attollere tandem
visa, aperire procul montes ac volvere fumum.

Themes
- a. The long and winding road brings me back to you.
- b. There is a time to smile and a time not to.
- c. Might doesn't always make right.
- d. The man has a sick sense of humor.
- e. Don't consult a crystal ball.

71. tamen renidere usque quaque te nollem:
nam risu inepto res ineptior nulla est.

72. tu ne quaesieris, scire nefas, quem mihi, quem tibi
finem di dederint, Leuconoe, nec Babylonios
temptaris numeros.

73. renidet ille. quidquid est, ubicumque est,
quodcumque agit, renidet: hunc habet morbum,
neque elegantem, ut arbitror, neque urbanum.

74. multas per gentes et multa per aequora vectus,
    advenio has miseras, frater, ad inferias,
    ut te postremo donarem munere mortis
    et mutam nequiquam adloquerer cinerem.

75. quid magis est saxo durum, quid mollius unda?
    dura tamen molli saxa cavantur aqua.

XIII Directions

Indicate the authors of the following pieces. Some author's names will be used more than once.

a. Catullus   b. Horace   c. Ovid   d. Phaedrus   e. Vergil

76. carpe diem, quam minimum credula postero.

77. "ante hos sex menses male" ait "dixisti mihi."
    respondit agnus: "equidem natus non eram."
    "pater hercle tuus" ille inquit "male dixit mihi;"
    atque ita correptum lacerat, iniusta nece.

78. nunc tamen interea haec, prisco quae more parentum
    tradita sunt tristi munere ad inferias,
    accipe fraterno multum manantia fletu,
    atque in perpetuum, frater, ave atque vale.

79. tempore difficiles veniunt ad aratra iuvenci,
    tempore lenta pati frena docentur equi.

80. ipse diem noctemque negat discernere caelo
    nec meminisse viae media Palinurus in unda.
    tres adeo incertos caeca caligine soles
    erramus pelago, totidem sine sidere noctes.
    quarto terra die primum se attollere tandem
    visa, aperire procul montes ac volvere fumum.

81. tamen renidere usque quaque te nollem:
    nam risu inepto res ineptior nulla est.

82. tu ne quaesieris, scire nefas, quem mihi, quem tibi
    finem di dederint, Leuconoe, nec Babylonios
    temptaris numeros.

83. renidet ille. quidquid est, ubicumque est,
    quodcumque agit, renidet: hunc habet morbum,
    neque elegantem, ut arbitror, neque urbanum.

84. multas per gentes et multa per aequora vectus,
   advenio has miseras, frater, ad inferias,
ut te postremo donarem munere mortis
   et mutam nequiquam adloquerer cinerem.

85. quid magis est saxo durum, quid mollius unda?
   dura tamen molli saxa cavantur aqua.

XIV Directions

*Select the word that does **NOT** belong in the group.*

86. a. rates   b. ignes   c. naves

87. a. mare   b. pelagus   c. terra

88. a. gurges   b. imber   c. hiems

89. a. nox   b. umida   c. tenebrae

90. a. sidus   b. dies   c. aetas

XV Directions

Match the meaning to the English derivative.

91. vis major   a. a substance to clean teeth

92. dentifrice   b. overwhelming force of nature that may exempt one from
                      the terms of a contract
93. emollient
                   c. to make an extract
94. remunerate
                   d. to compensate
95. excerpt
                   e. softening; soothing

****

96. allocution   a. a two-pronged spear

97. bident   b. not common; rarely seen

98. munificent   c. a formal address

99. impious   d. lacking reverence for God

100. scarce   e. very generous in giving

Stage 43 Test

PLEASE DO NOT WRITE ON THE TEST BOOKLET.
MARK ALL ANSWERS ON THE MACHINE SCORED ANSWER SHEET.

I   Directions

Tell to whom these statements refer. Use **a** *for the* **lady of Ephesus**, **b** *for the* **soldier**, **c** *for* **Turia**, *and* **d** *for* **Vespillo**.

1. quibus blanditiis impetraverat miles ut matrona vellet vivere, isdem etiam pudicitiam eius aggressus est.

2. matrona quaedam Ephesi tam notae erat pudicitiae, ut vicinarum quoque gentium feminas ad spectaculum sui evocaret.

3. proxima ergo nocte, cum miles, qui cruces asservabat, ne quis ad sepulturam corpus detraheret, notasset sibi lumen inter monumenta clarius fulgens et gemitum lugentis audisset, vitio gentis humanae concupiit scire, quis aut quid faceret.

4. homo qui inter cameram et tectum cubiculi celavit et ab exitio servatus est.

5. non recessit tamen miles, sed eadem exhortatione temptavit dare mulierculae cibum.

6. femina quae divortium propter orbitatem eius proposuit.

7. haec ergo cum virum extulisset, in conditorium etiam prosecuta est defunctum.

8. homo qui consilio uxoris divortii incensus est.

9. "malo mortuum impendere quam vivum occidere." secundum hanc orationem iubet ex arca corpus mariti sui tolli atque illi, quae vacabat, cruci affigi.

10. orbata es repente ante nuptiarum diem, utroque parente in rustica solitudine una occisis.

II   Directions

Select the correct answer based on the grammar of the previous quotes.

11. **In quote 1 what are the tense and mood of <u>impetraverat</u>?**
    a. imperfect indicative
    c. pluperfect indicative
    b. imperfect subjunctive
    d. pluperfect subjunctive

12. **In quote 2 what is the subjunctive use of <u>evocaret</u>?**
    a. positive purpose
    b. positive result
    c. positive indirect command

13. **In quote 3 what is the subjunctive use of <u>detraheret</u>?**

    a. negative purpose   b. negative result   c. negative indirect command

14. **In quote 3 what is the subjunctive use of <u>faceret</u>?**

    a. indirect question   b. indirect command   c. purpose clause

15. **In quote 4 what are the tense and voice of <u>servatus est</u>?**

    a. perfect active   c. pluperfect active
    b. perfect passive   d. pluperfect passive

16. **In quote 5 what is the case of <u>eadem</u>?**

    a. nominative   b. genitive   c. dative   d. accusative   e. ablative

17. **In quote 7 what are the tense and mood of <u>extulisset</u>?**

    a. imperfect indicative   c. pluperfect indicative
    b. imperfect subjunctive   d. pluperfect subjunctive

18. **In quote 9 what are the tense and voice of <u>impendere</u>?**

    a. present active   c. perfect active
    b. present passive   d. perfect passive

19. **In quote 9 what are the tense and voice of <u>affigi</u>?**

    a. present active   c. perfect active
    b. present passive   d. perfect passive

20. **In quote 10 what are the case and number of <u>nuptiarum</u>?**

    a. nominative singular   c. genitive plural
    b. accusative singular   d. accusative plural

III   Directions

Indicate whether the following culture statements are true or false by marking **a** *for* **true** *and* **b** *for* **false**.

21. It is a proven fact that the first Roman divorce occurred in 230 B.C.

22. There was a religious ban on divorce in ancient Rome.

23. Divorce reached its peak in the first century A.D. and declined later.

24. There was no social stigma attached to a divorced spouse.

25. Much is known about divorce among the rich and poor in Rome.

26. Some husbands stayed with their wives in order not to return the **dos**.

27. It was common to marry several times in ancient Rome.

28. **Univirae** were highly respected by the Romans.

29. Everyone was allowed to visit the Temple of Pudicitia.

30. It was traditional for a **univira** to help a bride undress on her wedding night.

IV Directions

Select the Latin sentence that correctly translates the English sentence.

31. **The priest ordered the citizens to pray to the immortal gods.**
    a. sacerdotes cives dixerunt deos immortales precari.
    b. sacerdos civibus imperavit ut deos immortales precarentur.

32. **We were resisting fiercely in order that we not be overpowered by the barbarians.**
    a. ferociter resistebamus ne a barbaris superaremur.
    b. tam ferociter resistebamus ut a barbaris non superaremur.

33. **I hear that the horses are being exercised today.**
    a. audivi equos heri exercuisse.
    b. audio equos hodie exerceri.

34. **I hoped that the girl would write to us.**
    a. speravi puellam ad nos scripturam esse.
    b. spero puellas ad nos scripturam esse.

35. **We said that many barbarians had fallen in battle.**
    a. multos barbaros dicimus in proelio cadere.
    b. multos barbaros diximus in proelio cecidisse.

V Directions

Identify the following statements as **a** = *the supposed reason for Roman marriage,* **b** = *reasons for divorce,* **c** = *a reason to marry or divorce, and* **d** = *ways of obtaining a divorce.*

36. Husband says in front of witnesses **tuas res tibi habet**.

37. Objectionable behavior.

38. Send written notification.

39. To produce children.

40. Political reasons.

41. Demand return of house keys.

42. Quarreling and disagreements.

43. Husband and wife make a joint declaration in front of witnesses.

44. Childlessness.

45. To marry someone wealthier or from a more powerful family.

VI Directions

Match these words to their Latin synonyms.

46. colloquium   a. igitur

47. coniunx   b. festinare

48. contendere   c. aedificare

49. ergo   d. uxor

50. exstruere   e. sermo

VII Directions

Select the correct form of the infinitive to complete the sentence.
    a. mittere   b. mitti   c. missurum esse

51. **ducem auxilium mox _____ speramus.**
We hope that the leader <u>sends</u> help soon.

52. **ducem auxilium mox _____ speravimus.**
We hoped that the leader <u>would send</u> help soon.

53. **auxilium a duce mox _____ speramus.**
We hope that help <u>is</u> soon <u>sent</u> by the leader.

               ****

    a. vexare   b. vexari   c. vexavisse   d. vexatas esse   e. vexaturos esse

54. **scit multas provincias a latronibus _____.**
He knows that many provinces <u>have been troubled</u> by bandits.

55. **scit multas provincias a latronibus _____.**
He knows that many provinces <u>are troubled</u> by bandits.

56. **scit latrones multas provincias _____.**
He knows that bandits <u>trouble</u> many provinces.

57. **scit latrones multas provincias _____.**
He knows that bandits <u>will trouble</u> many provinces.

58. **scit latrones multas provincias _____.**
He knows that bandits <u>have troubled</u> many provinces.

****

    a. servatam esse   b. servaturos esse   c. servavisse

59. **credo milites fidem _____.**

I believe that the soldiers <u>will keep</u> their word.

60. **credo milites fidem _____.**

I believe that the soldiers <u>kept</u> their word.

61. **credo fidem a militibus _____.**

I believe that their word <u>was kept</u> by the soldiers.

VIII Directions

Indicate whether the following sentences contain an indirect statement or an indirect question. Use **a** *for* **indirect statement** *and* **b** *for* **indirect question**.

62. nauta dicit se navem mox refecturum esse.

63. ubi senex gemmas celaverit, milites agnoscere volunt.

64. quo modo imperator moreretur, nemo scivit.

65. nuntii villas negant deletas esse.

66. haruspices cognoscere conabuntur num omina bona sint.

67. centurio hostes dicit constitisse.

68. nescio quare Imperator Agricolam revocaverit.

IX Directions

Indicate the tense of the <u>underlined</u> words.

    a. present   b. imperfect   c. future   d. perfect

69. nauta dicit se navem mox <u>refecturum</u> esse.

70. ubi senex gemmas <u>celaverit</u>, milites agnoscere volunt.

71. quo modo imperator <u>moreretur</u>, nemo scivit.

72. nuntii villas negant <u>deletas</u> esse.

73. haruspices cognoscere <u>conabuntur</u> num omina bona sint.

74. centurio hostes dicit <u>constitisse</u>.

75. nescio quare Imperator Agricolam <u>revocaverit</u>.

X   Directions

Select the correct translations for the following conditional sentences.

76. **si in eodem loco mansisses, periculum vitavisses.**

77. **si in eodem loco maneas, periculum vites.**

78. **si in eodem loco maneres, periculum vitares.**

   a. If you should stay in the same place, you would avoid the danger.
   b. If you had stayed in the same place, you would have avoided the danger.
   c. If you were staying in the same place, you would avoid the danger.

****

79. **si rex essem, non in hac villa laborarem.**

80. **si rex sim, non in hac villa laborem.**

81. **si rex fuissem, non in hac villa laboravissem.**

   a. If I had been king, I would not have worked in this house.
   b. If I were king, I would not work in this house.
   c. If I should be king, I would not work in this house.

****

82. **si illud iterum feceris, te puniam.**
   a. If you do that again, I will punish you.
   b. If you should do that again, I would punish you.

****

83. **si milites urbem oppugnent, facile eam capiant.**

84. **si milites urbem oppugnarent, facile eam caperent.**

85. **si milites urbem oppugnavissent, facile eam cepissent.**

   a. If the soldiers should attack the city, they would easily capture it.
   b. If the soldiers had attacked the city, they would have easily captured it.
   c. If the soldiers were attacking the city, they would easily capture it.

XI Directions

Match these culture terms to their definitions.

86. manus

87. sine manu

88. univira

89. dos

90. one condition to be met before the divorce was final

a. payment by bride to husband at the time of the marriage

b. a woman married only once

c. legal control by the husband

d. prove that they intended to live separately

e. the type of legal control where either spouse could divorce the other

****

91. Spurius Carvilius

92. Gaius Petronius Arbiter

93. laudatio

94. Dido

95. one condition to be met before divorce was final

a. **arbiter elegantiae** of Nero

b. supposed **univira**: a famous queen

c. demonstrate that they thought the marriage was finished

d. first person to divorce because of childlessness

e. speech in praise of a dead person

XII Directions

Match the meaning to the English derivative.

96. aggression

97. juxtaposition

98. illumination

99. negation

100. option

a. being side by side

b. a choosing; a choice

c. an unprovoked attack

d. enlightenment; instruction

e. a negative answer; denial

Stage 44 Test

PLEASE DO NOT WRITE ON THE TEST BOOKLET.
MARK ALL ANSWERS ON THE MACHINE SCORED ANSWER SHEET.

I Directions

Identify the speaker or the person(s) to whom the quotations refer.

   a. bystanders   b. Daedalus   c. Icarus   d. Minos

1. "terras licet" inquit "et undas
   obstruat, at caelum certe patet; ibimus illac!"

2. omnia possideat, non possidet aera.

3. dixit et ignotas animum dimittit in artes,
   naturamque novat.

4. stabat et, ignarus sua se tractare pericla,

5. "moneo, ne, si demissior ibis,
   unda gravet pennas, si celsior, ignis adurat.
   inter utrumque vola!"

6. captabat plumas, flavam modo pollice ceram
   mollibat,

7. hos aliquis, tremula dum captat harundine pisces,
   aut pastor baculo stivave innixus arator
   vidit et obstipuit, quique aethera carpere possent
   credidit esse deos.

8. cum puer audaci coepit gaudere volatu
   deseruitque ducem, caelique cupidine tractus
   altius egit iter.

9. tabuerant cerae; nudos quatit ille lacertos,
   remigioque carens non ullas percipit auras.
   oraque caerulea patrium clamantia nomen
   excipiuntur aqua, quae nomen traxit ab illo.

10. dixit, "ubi es? qua te regione requiram?"

II Directions

Match the meaning to the English derivative.

11.	abscond	a.	growth, especially by addition
12.	caret	b.	a gradual increase in loudness
13.	conjunction	c.	to go away hastily and secretly
14.	accretion	d.	association; a combination
15.	crescendo	e.	a mark used to show where something is to be added

****

16.	felicitations	a.	a taking advantage of friendship
17.	imposition	b.	a formal order, request
18.	superimpose	c.	congratulations
19.	requisition	d.	permit to do something
20.	license	e.	to lay something on top of something else

III Directions

Match the definitions to the literary devices.

21.	alliteration	a.	a term used to characterize someone
22.	assonance	b.	word order device: $A_1 A_2 N_2 N_1$
23.	bracketing/framing	c.	repetition of vowel sounds
24.	chiasmus	d.	repetition of consonant sounds
25.	epithet	e.	word order device: $A_1 N_1 N_2 A_2$

****

26.	hendiadys	a.	sound of word expresses its meaning
27.	imagery	b.	an explicit comparison using *like* or *as*
28.	metonomy	c.	one idea expressed through two words
29.	onomatopoeia	d.	a word is used to suggest another with which it is closely related
30.	simile	e.	the use of descriptions to convey the meaning

****

31. synchesis	a. arrangement of words to suggest the meaning visibly
32. syncope	b. a part used to represent the whole
33. synecdoche	c. interlocking word order
34. transferred epithet	d. the shortening of a word to fit the meter
35. word picture	e. application of an adjective to a noun when it really refers to another noun

IV Directions

Identify the literary device found in the following quotations.

a. alliteration b. assonance c. chiasmus d. epithet e. hendiadys

36. Daedalus interea Creten longumque perosus exilium

37. <u>n</u>aturamque <u>n</u>ovat. <u>n</u>am ponit in ordine pennas,

38. ore renidenti modo, quas vaga moverat aura

39. <u>a</u>nte volat, comitique timet, velut <u>a</u>les, <u>a</u>b <u>a</u>lto

40.   et iam Iunonia laeva
    parte Samos (fuerant Delosque Parosque relictae),

****

a. simile   c. syncope   e. word picture
b. synchesis   d. transferred epithet

41. geminas opifex libravit in alas

42. oraque caerulea patrium clamantia nomen

43. cum puer audaci coepit gaudere volatu

44. inter opus monitusque genae maduere seniles

45.   velut ales, ab alto
    quae teneram prolem produxit in aera nido;

V Directions

Identify the grammar point found in each line.

46. **cum puer audaci coepit <u>gaudere</u> volatu**
    a. complementary infinitive   c. verb of an indirect statement
    b. ablative noun

47. **deseruitque ducem, <u>caeli</u>que cupidine tractus**

    a. genitive   b. ablative   c. dative

48. **deseruitque ducem, caelique cupidine <u>tractus</u>**

    a. present active participle   c. perfect passive participle
    b. perfect active participle

49. **<u>altius</u> egit iter. rapidi vicinia solis**

    a. comparative adjective   b. comparative adverb

50. **<u>tabuerant</u> cerae; nudos quatit ille lacertos,**

    a. present active   c. perfect active
    b. imperfect active   d. pluperfect active

51. **<u>remigio</u>que carens non ullas percipit auras.**

    a. accusative   b. ablative   c. dative

52. **oraque caerulea patrium <u>clamantia</u> nomen**

    a. present active participle   c. perfect passive participle
    b. perfect active participle

53. **tabuerant cerae; nudos <u>quatit</u> ille lacertos,**

    a. present active   c. perfect active
    b. imperfect active   d. pluperfect active

54. **<u>deseruit</u>que ducem, caelique cupidine tractus**

    a. present active   c. perfect active
    b. imperfect active   d. pluperfect active

55. **altius egit iter. rapidi vicinia <u>solis</u>**

    a. genitive   b. dative   c. accusative

VI Directions

Read the following quotations and indicate whether they deal with imagery or foreshadowing by using **a** *for* **imagery** *and* **b** *for* **foreshadowing**.

56.   ignotas animum dimittit in artes,
naturamque novat.

57.   sic rustica quondam
fistula disparibus paulatim surgit avenis.

58. inter opus monitusque genae maduere seniles,
et patriae tremuere manus.

59.   nam ponit in ordine pennas,
ut clivo crevisse putes;

60.   dedit oscula nato
      non iterum repetenda suo

61.   velut ales, ab alto
      quae teneram prolem produxit in aera nido,

VII Directions

Match the artist or poet to his appropriate time period.

62. Allegrini	a.	6th century B.C.
63. W. H. Auden	b.	1st century A.D.
64. Michael Ayrton	c.	16th century A.D.
65. Pieter Bruegel	d.	20th century A.D.
66. Greek vase		
67. Ovid		
68. wall-painting		

VIII Directions

Match the poet to the quotation of his work.

    a. W. H. Auden   b. Ovid

69. About suffering they were never wrong,
     The Old Masters: how well they understood
     Its human position; how it takes place …
     They never forgot
     That even the dreadful martyrdom must run its course

70. and he instructed his son, "I warn you, Icarus," he said, "to fly in the middle
     course lest, if you fly too low, the water may weigh down your wings, and if
     you fly too high, the sun may burn them."

IX Directions

Indicate the idiomatic use of **solvere** *that correctly finishes these sentences.*

    a. aenigma solvere
    b. catenas ex aliquo solvere
    c. margaritam in aceto solvere
    d. navem solvere

71. nautae navem paraverunt et ita _____ poterant.

72. heros ianuam carceris fregit et _____ poterat.

73. magistra mathematici _____ non poterat.

74. medicus hominem _____ iussit ut medicinam raram faceret.

****

    a. pecuniam solvere
    b. vino solutus
    c. votum solvere

75. homo pauper mercatori denarios duos dedit et ita _____ poterat.

76. proelio victo, victor deo Marti templum aedificavit et ita _____ poterat.

77. homo fessus, _____, dormire poterat.

X Directions

Read the following sentences and indicate which grammar point or stylistic technique is being demonstrated.

    a. ellipsis   b. historic present   c. indirect statement   d. syncope

78. rex credebat leones equum occisuros esse.

79. nos in urbe, vos prope mare habitatis.

80. fur per fenestram intravit; omnia tacita erant; subito sonitum audit; latrat canis.

81. agricola querebatur multam aquam per hortum suum fluxisse.

82. illo proelio multi barbari periere.

83. dum mater cenam parat, pater dormivit.

84. centum me tetigere manus.

85. enumerat miles vulnera, pastor oves.

XI Directions

Match the meaning to the English derivative.

86. aspect   a. inhabitant of the earth

87. conjugal   b. excessive desire

88. cupidity   c. bond, tie

89. tellurian   d. referring to a marital relationship

90. vinculum   e. an appearance, a way of looking at something

XII Directions

Match these poetic characters and places to their definitions.

91. Crete   a. son of the master craftsman

92. Daedalus   b. island of the labyrinth

93. Icarus   c. constellation of the Great Hunter

94. Minos   d. famous craftsman and inventor

95. Orion   e. king who imprisoned Daedalus and Icarus

****

96. arator   a. shepherd who leaned on his staff

97. Delos   b. fisherman with trembling hook

98. Paros   c. plowman who watched the fall

99. pastor   d. island of Apollo

100. piscator   e. island famed for marble

Stage 45 Test

PLEASE DO NOT WRITE ON THE TEST BOOKLET.
MARK ALL ANSWERS ON THE MACHINE SCORED ANSWER SHEET.

I   Directions

Read the following poem. (The underlined words indicate adjective–noun pairings, where the words are not adjacent.)

passer, deliciae meae puellae,	1
quicum ludere, quem in **sinu** tenere,	2
cui primum **digitum** dare **adpetenti**	3
et <u>acres</u> solet incitare <u>morsus</u>,	4
cum **desiderio** meo **nitenti**	5
carum nescio quid libet iocari,	6
et **solaciolum** sui doloris,	7
credo, et cum <u>gravis</u> **acquiescit** <u>ardor</u>,	8
tecum ludere sicut ipsa **possem**	9
et <u>tristes</u> animi **levare** <u>curas</u>!	10

Words and Phrases

quicum - with whom
sinu: sinus - lap
digitum: digitus - finger
adpetenti - to peck at
solet: goes with **ludere**, **tenere**, **dare**, and **incitare**
incitare - arouse
morsus: morsus - peck, bite
desiderio: desiderium - beloved, sweetheart

nitenti: nitens - radiant
carum nescio quid libet iocari - enjoys some affectionate joke
solaciolum - as a comfort
acquiescit: acquiescere - lessen, be relieved
ardor - passion
possem - I wish I could
levare - lighten, lessen

II   Directions

Select the correct answer based on the content and the grammar of the poem.

1. **What is the meter of this piece?**
   a. dactylic hexameter   b. elegiac couplet   c. hendecasyllabic

2. **In line 2 where is the sparrow when Lesbia is playing with it?**
   a. in her lap   b. on her finger   c. on her head

3. **In line 2 what is the form of <u>tenere</u>?**
   a. syncope   b. present active infinitive   c. present passive infinitive

4. **In line 3 what does Lesbia use to play with her sparrow?**

   a. her head   b. her finger   c. her teeth

5. **In line 3 what type of participle is <u>adpetenti</u>?**

   a. present active   b. perfect passive   c. future active

6. **In line 4 what does the bird do to play with its mistress?**

   a. peck at her   b. sing to her   c. joke with her

7. **In line 6 what is the form of <u>iocari</u>?**

   a. syncope   b. present active infinitive   c. present passive infinitive

8. **In lines 5–8 what does Catullus suggest is happening?**

   a. that the bird plays with Lesbia to lessen its own grief
   b. that Lesbia plays with the bird to lessen her own grief
   c. that Lesbia plays with the bird to take her away from her new love

9. **In lines 9–10 what is Catullus' hope?**

   a. that he could play with Lesbia as Lesbia plays with her bird
   b. that Lesbia would play with him as she does with the bird
   c. that he could play a game to lighten his sad cares

10. **In line 9 what is the case of <u>te</u> in <u>tecum</u>?**

   a. nominative   b. genitive   c. dative   d. accusative   e. ablative

III Directions

Match the name of the meter to its scansion pattern and then to examples of it from the Catullan poems you have read.

   a. elegiac couplet   b. hendecasyllabic

11. ⏓ – | – ⏑ ⏑ | – ⏑ | – ⏑ | – ⏓

12. Line 1   – ⏑ ⏑ | – ⏑ ⏑ | – ⏑ ⏑ | – ⏑ ⏑ | – ⏑ ⏑ | – ⏓
    Line 2   – ⏑ ⏑ | – ⏑ ⏑ | – ‖ – ⏑ ⏑ | – ⏑ ⏑ | ⏑

13. da mi basia mille, deinde centum,
    dein mille altera, dein secunda centum,

14. nunc te cognovi: quare etsi impensius uror,
    multo mi tamen es vilior et levior.

15. lugete, o Veneres Cupidinesque,
    et quantum est hominum venustiorum!

IV Directions

Match the name of the person to the pronoun or adjective to which it refers.

    a. Catullus   b. Lesbia   c. Lesbia's admirer   d. Iuppiter

[16]ille [17]mi par esse deo videtur,

ille, si fas est, superare divos,

qui sedens adversus identidem [18]te
    spectat et audit

                ****

nulli se dicit [19]mulier mea nubere malle

    quam [20]mihi, non si se [21]*** ipse petat.

                ****

    a. Catullus   b. Lesbia   c. passer   d. tenebrae Orci

[22]quem plus [23]illa oculis [24]suis amabat

nam mellitus erat suamque norat

                ****

at [25]vobis male sit, malae *******

****, quae omnia bella devoratis:

tam bellum [26]mihi passerem abstulistis.

o factum male! o miselle passer!

[27]tua nunc opera, [28]meae puellae

V   Directions

If the Catullus–Lesbia relationship may be characterized by the five following descriptions, indicate to which description the listed excerpts belong.

    a. the initial infatuation and first experiences with Lesbia
    b. the total joy in the relationship
    c. the coy love poem centered around a pet
    d. the disillusionment

29. nulli se dicit mulier mea nubere malle
        quam mihi, non si se Iuppiter ipse petat.
    dicit: sed mulier cupido quod dicit amanti,
        in vento et rapida scribere oportet aqua.

30. ille mi par esse deo videtur,
    ille, si fas est, superare divos,
    qui sedens adversus identidem te
        spectat et audit

31. vivamus, mea Lesbia, atque amemus
    rumoresque senum severiorum
    omnes unius aestimemus assis!

32. nam mellitus erat suamque norat
    ipsam tam bene quam puella matrem,
    nec sese a gremio illius movebat,
    sed circumsiliens modo huc modo illuc
    ad solam dominam usque pipiabat;

33. dilexi tum te non tantum ut vulgus amicam,
        sed pater ut gnatos diligit et generos.
    nunc te cognovi: quare etsi impensius uror,
        multo mi tamen es vilior et levior.

34. lingua sed torpet, tenuis sub artus
    flamma demanat, sonitu suopte
    tintinant aures, gemina teguntur
        lumina nocte.

35. passer mortuus est meae puellae,
    passer, deliciae meae puellae,
    quem plus illa oculis suis amabat.

VI Directions

Match the dative use to a Latin example of it.

36. liber mihi legendus est.   a. indirect object

37. villa magnifica Catullo est.   b. object of a special verb

38. mater liberis librum dedit.   c. double dative

39. liber auxilio magno magistrae erat.   d. dative of possession

40. legatus homini innocenti credidit.   e. dative of agent

VII Directions

Match the philosophy expressed to the Latin quotation.

    a. The pain of love can cut like a knife or sharp instrument.
    b. Life is short; death is forever.
    c. Women are fickle, and their loyalty can change as quickly as the weather.
    d. Idle hands are the devil's workshop.
    e. The journey to the Underworld is the final destination.

41. otium, Catulle, tibi molestum est:
    otio exsultas nimiumque gestis:
    otium et reges prius et beatas
        perdidit urbes.

42. soles occidere et redire possunt:
    nobis, cum semel occidit brevis lux,
    nox est perpetua una dormienda.

43. qui nunc it per iter tenebricosum
    illuc, unde negant redire quemquam.

44. dicit: sed mulier cupido quod dicit amanti,
        in vento et rapida scribere oportet aqua.

45. nec meum respectet, ut ante, amorem,
    qui illius culpa cecidit velut prati
    ultimi flos, praetereunte postquam
        tactus aratro est.

VIII Directions

In each sentence, state if the participle is **a** *gerund or* **b** *gerundive.*

46. nobis villa aedificanda est.

47. multi homines ad audiendum aderant.

48. puer artem cantandi carminis discere conabatur.

49. iuvenis ad epistulam legendam consedit.

50. diu laborando, pecuniam multam meruit.

IX Directions

Match the subjunctive name to its clue or translation.

51. speaker encourages himself or others   a. deliberative

52. speaker wonders what to do   b. hortatory

53. Let him …   c. jussive – 3rd person

54. 1st person present subjunctive   d. jussive – 2nd person

55. a type of command

56. Let us …

57. Let them …

X Directions

Indicate the type of subjunctive use found in the following sentences.

58. statim discedamus.   a. deliberative

59. desinas queri.   b. hortatory

60. quo fugiam?   c. jussive – 3rd person

61. fiat lux!   d. jussive – 2nd person

62. litteram scribam.

63. quid cogitem?

64. laetus sis!

65. libros legant!

XI Directions

Match the correct translation to the Latin sentence.

66. libros legant! a. Let me read the books!

67. libros legas! b. Let him read the books!

68. quos libros legam? c. Let them read the books!

69. libros legam! d. You should read the books!

70. libros legat! e. What books should I read?

XII Directions

Match the correct definition to the culture term.

71. Clodia a. Greek island

72. Lesbia b. husband of Clodia

73. Lesbos c. fashionable Roman lady

74. Q. Caecilius Metellus Celer d. pseudonym of Catullus' lover

75. Sappho e. Greek poetess of the 7th century B.C.

****

76. chief Roman lyric poets a. written to be recited or read

77. epic poetry b. Horace and Catullus

 c. songs that were accompanied by music

78. lyric poetry d. melodic poetry written in an intensely personal and direct style

79. Greek lyric poetry

80. Latin lyric poetry e. objective representation of a subject as opposed to personal sentiments

XIII Directions

*Indicate whether the following statements about Clodia would be **a** apparent facts or **b** negative rumors.*

81. She murdered her husband.

82. She was interested in politics.

83. She chose an independent role in society.

84. She committed incest with her brother.

85. She had had several lovers.

XIV Directions

Match the meaning to the English derivative.

86.	candid	a.	a covering; shell, hide, etc.
87.	feeble	b.	womanhood
88.	muliebrity	c.	impartial; outspoken
89.	otiose	d.	weak; infirm
90.	integument	e.	idle; indolent

****

91.	tenuous	a.	a person under the patronage of another
92.	revile	b.	a finding out
93.	protégé	c.	unsubstantial; flimsy
94.	detection	d.	cannot be bribed
95.	incorruptible	e.	to use abusive language in speaking about

XV Directions

Match the Latin word to its antonym.

96.	dare	a.	accipere
97.	demittere	b.	adiuvare
98.	impedire	c.	desinere
99.	incipere	d.	gaudere
100.	lugere	e.	tollere

Stage 46 Test

PLEASE DO NOT WRITE ON THE TEST BOOKLET.
MARK ALL ANSWERS ON THE MACHINE SCORED ANSWER SHEET.

I Directions

Read the following passage.

duo sunt enim crimina una in muliere summorum facinorum, auri quod	1
sumptum a Clodia dicitur, et veneni quod eiusdem Clodiae necandae	2
causa parasse Caelium **criminantur**. aurum sumpsit, ut dicitis, quod L.	3
Luccei servis daret, **per quos** Alexandrinus Dio qui tum apud Lucceium	4
habitabat necaretur. magnum crimen vel in legatis **insidiandis** vel in	5
servis ad hospitem domini necandum **sollicitandis**, plenum sceleris	6
consilium, plenum audaciae! quo quidem in crimine primum illud	7
requiro, dixeritne Clodiae quam ob rem aurum sumeret, an non dixerit?	8
si non dixit, cur dedit? si dixit, eodem se **conscientiae** scelere **devinxit**.	9

Words and Phrases

criminantur: criminari - accuse
per quos - by whom
insidiandis: insidiari - plot against
sollicitandis: sollicitare - incite
conscientiae: conscientia - joint knowledge with someone else, awareness
devinxit: devincire - attach, bind

II Directions

Select the correct answer based on the content and the grammar of the passage.

1. **In line 1 we read that two charges _____.**

    a. deal with minor crimes   b. deal with one woman   c. deal with a mule

2. **In line 1 the degree of <u>summorum</u> is _____.**

    a. positive   b. comparative   c. superlative

3. **In lines 1–3 we learn that _____.**

    a. gold was taken from Clodia and Caelius prepared poison for her
    b. Clodia took the gold and prepared poison for Caelius
    c. gold was taken from Clodia and that Clodius prepared poison for Caelius

4. **In line 2 the case of <u>eiusdem</u> is _____.**

    a. nominative   b. genitive   c. dative   d. accusative   e. ablative

5. **In line 2 the form and use of <u>necandae</u> are _____.**

   a. gerund – purpose   b. gerundive – obligation   c. gerundive – purpose

6. **In lines 3–5 we learn that the gold was stolen _____.**

   a. to kill Lucceius

   b. to pay slaves of L. Lucceius to kill Alexandrinus Dio

   c. to pay slaves of Alexandrinus Dio to kill L. Lucceius

7. **In lines 4–5 Alexandrinus Dio _____.**

   a. provided a home for Lucceius

   b. provided a home for the slaves of Lucceius

   c. lived at the home of Lucceius

8. **In line 5 the tense and mood of <u>necaretur</u> are _____.**

   a. present indicative   c. imperfect indicative

   b. present subjunctive   d. imperfect subjunctive

9. **In lines 5–7 we learn that it was a serious charge _____.**

   a. to plot against ambassadors and to incite the slaves to kill a household guest

   b. to have the ambassadors plot and to kill the slaves of a household guest

   c. to plot against ambassadors and to have a household guest kill the slaves of the master

10. **In line 6 the form and use of <u>necandum</u> are _____.**

   a. gerund – purpose   c. gerundive – purpose

   b. gerund – noun   d. gerundive – adjective

11. **In line 6 the form and use of <u>sollicitandis</u> are _____.**

   a. gerund – purpose   c. gerundive – purpose

   b. gerund – noun   d. gerundive – adjective

12. **In lines 6–7 <u>plenum … audaciae</u> is an example of _____.**

   a. chiasmus   b. framing   c. parallelism   d. synchesis

13. **In lines 7–8 Cicero wants to know whether or not _____.**

   a. Caelius asked permission to take the gold

   b. Caelius told Clodia why he needed the gold

   c. Clodia told Caelius why she needed the gold

14. **In line 8 the tense and mood of <u>dixerit</u> are _____.**

   a. perfect subjunctive   c. pluperfect indicative

   b. future perfect indicative d. imperfect subjunctive

15. **In the last sentence Cicero states that _____.**

   a. it did not matter whether he said it or not

   b. he was still guilty because of his awareness

   c. she was still guilty because of her awareness

III Directions

Select the correct form of the relative pronoun to replace the underlined word.

16. **puellam vidi. vir puellae donum dedit.**

    a. quae   b. quam   c. cui   d. cuius

17. **puer ad villam cucurrit. villa ardebat.**

    a. quae   b. quam   c. cui   d. cuius

18. **puellas vidimus. mater puellarum ridebat.**

    a. quae   b. quas   c. quibus   d. quarum

19. **nemo scivit quid vir factum esset. vir montem cecidit.**

    a. qui   b. quem   c. quo   d. cui

20. **nos saxa gravia vidimus. saxa a liberis iaciebantur.**

    a. quae   b. quod   c. quibus   d. quorum

21. **fur atrium tacite intravit. fure viso, canis latravit.**

    a. qui   b. quem   c. quo   d. cui

22. **in media urbe stabat templum. simulatque templum intravi, attonitus constiti.**

    a. quem   b. quam   c. quod   d. quae

23. **homines clamare coeperunt. clamoribus hominum excitatus, surrexi.**

    a. quae   b. quod   c. quibus   d. quorum

24. **rex epistulam dictavit. nuntius Imperatori epistulam tradidit.**

    a. quem   b. quam   c. quod   d. quae

25. **Quintus "Salvium perfidiae accuso," inquit. verbis auditis, Salvius tacuit.**

    a. quae   b. quod   c. quibus   d. quorum

IV Directions

Match the definition to the correct person.

26. Caelius
27. Cicero
28. Clodia
29. Clodius
30. Crassus

a. person whom the defendant had allegedly attempted to poison
b. multimillionaire who spoke on behalf of the defendant
c. Rome's leading orator
d. had a bitter and long-running feud with one of the defense attorneys
e. the defendant who was charged with owing money and attempted poisoning

V Directions

Indicate the rhetorical devices found in the following examples.

       a. anaphora   b. ellipsis   c. synchesis   d. syncope   e. tricolon crescens

31. aurum sumptum (est) a Clodia, venenum quaesitum (est) quod Clodiae daretur.

32. horum duorum criminum **video auctorem**, **video fontem**, **video certum nomen et caput**.

33. quae si se aurum Caelio commodasse non dicit.

34. **ideo**ne ego pacem Pyrrhi diremi ut tu amorum turpissimorum cotidie foedera ferires, **ideo** aquam adduxi ut ea tu inceste uterere, **ideo** viam munivi ut eam tu alienis viris comitata celebrares?

35. quae patrem complexa triumphantem ab inimico tribuno plebei de curru detrahi passa non est?

VI Directions

Indicate the persons referred to in the following passages.

       a. Appius Claudius Caecus   c. Clodia   e. Q. Metellus
       b. Caelius   d. Clodius

36. "adulter, impudicus, sequester"

37. quod quidem facerem vehementius, nisi intercederent mihi inimicitiae cum istius mulieris <u>viro</u> – <u>fratrem</u> volui dicere; semper hic erro.

38. qui profecto, si exstiterit, sic aget ac sic loquetur: mulier, quid tibi cum Caelio, quid cum homine adulescentulo, quid cum alieno?

39. muliere non solum nobili verum etiam nota

40. non denique modo te **** matrimonium tenuisse sciebas, clarissimi ac fortissimi viri patriaeque amantissimi, qui simul ac pedem limine extulerat, omnis prope civis virtute, gloria, dignitate superabat?

Indicate the grammar points found in the following lines.

nullum est enim fundamentum horum **criminum**, nullae sedes; voces sunt contumeliosae temere **ab irato accusatore** nullo auctore **emissae**.

41. **What is the case of criminum?**

    a. nominative   b. genitive   c. dative   d. accusative   e. ablative

42. **What is the use of ab irato accusatore?**

    a. ablative of agent   b. ablative of means   c. dative of agent

43. **What type of participle is emissae?**

    a. present active   b. perfect active   c. perfect passive   d. future active

****

auro opus fuit

44. **What is the case of auro?**

    a. nominative   b. genitive   c. dative   d. accusative   e. ablative

****

necare **eandem** voluit

45. **What is the case of eandem?**

    a. nominative   b. genitive   c. dative   d. accusative   e. ablative

****

magnum rursus odium video cum crudelissimo discidio **exstitisse**.

46. **What is the form of exstitisse?**

    a. perfect active indicative   c. perfect active infinitive
    b. perfect active participle   d. perfect active subjunctive

****

res est omnis in hac causa nobis, iudices, cum Clodia, muliere non solum **nobili** verum etiam nota; de qua ego nihil dicam nisi **depellendi** criminis causa.

47. **What is the case of nobili?**

    a. nominative   b. genitive   c. dative   d. accusative   e. ablative

48. **What is the form of depellendi?**

    a. present active participle   b. gerund   c. gerundive

49. **What is the use of depellendi?**

    a. an adjective   b. purpose   c. noun

****

nunc **agam** modice nec longius **progrediar** quam me mea fides et causa ipsa **coget**.

50. **What are the tense and mood of the three verbs?**

    a. future indicative   b. present subjunctive   c. present indicative

****

aliquis mihi ab inferis **excitandus est** ex barbatis illis

51. **What are the form and use of <u>excitandus est</u>?**

    a. gerund – noun   b. gerundive – obligation   c. gerundive – purpose

****

exsistat igitur ex hac ipsa familia aliquis ac potissimum Caecus ille.

52. **What is the subjunctive use of the verb?**

    a. hortatory   b. jussive   c. deliberative

****

ideo aquam adduxi ut **ea** tu inceste uterere

53. **What is the case of the boldface pronoun?**

    a. nominative   b. genitive   c. dative   d. accusative   e. ablative

****

sed quid ego, iudices, ita gravem personam induxi ut verear ne se idem Appius repente **convertat** et Caelium incipiat **accusare** illa sua gravitate censoria?

54. **What is the use of <u>convertat</u>?**

    a. clause of fear   b. result clause   c. purpose clause

55. **What is the use of <u>accusare</u>?**

    a. syncope   b. complementary infinitive   c. verb of an indirect statement

VIII Directions

*Indicate whether the following culture statements are true or false by marking **a** for **true** and **b** for **false**.*

56. Court cases concerning Roman citizens were held in the open air in the Forum Romanum near the Temple of Castor and Pollux.

57. An orator needed a sound foundation in his knowledge of the law, but more especially great skill in the preparation, expression, and delivery of his case.

58. Because Cicero was very successful in arousing the emotions of jurors and spectators, he often gave the concluding speech in the plaintiff's case.

59. Cicero was not the first Roman to rise to the highest rank of Roman politics through oratory alone.

60. The Romans felt that the original aim of rhetoric was to give effectiveness to public speaking.

IX Directions

Match the definition to the culture term.

61.	absolvo	a.	voting tablet used to convict a defendant
62.	condemno	b.	jurors
63.	corona	c.	crimes involving violence and intimidation
64.	de vi	d.	voting tablet used to acquit a defendant
65.	iudices	e.	circle of curious spectators at a trial

****

66.	iuris consultus	a.	presiding magistrate at the court
67.	orator	b.	drawing of lots to select jurors
		c.	man who studied the legal aspects of the case and gave his opinion
68.	praetor urbanus		
		d.	courts for crimes committed by members of the upper classes
69.	quaestiones		
70.	sortitio	e.	person who presented the case in court

X Directions

Indicate the subjunctive uses found in the following sentences.

a. conditional   c. cum clause   e. purpose
b. clause of fearing   d. indirect question

71. amici tui timebant ne interfectus esses.

72. si diligentius laboravissem, dominus me liberavisset.

73. iudex rogavit quantam pecuniam mercator mihi pollicitus esset.

74. Cicero crimina exponit ut gravitatem causae intellegamus.

75. cum victimae sacrificatae essent, pontifex pauca verba dixit.

XI Directions

Select the correct translation for the following sentences.

76. **amici tui timebant ne interfectus esses.**
    a. Our friends were afraid that you had been killed.
    b. Your friends were afraid that you had been killed.

77. **si diligentius laboravissem, dominus me liberavisset.**
    a. If I had worked more diligently, my master would have freed me.
    b. If I were working more diligently, my master would free me.

78. **iudex rogavit quantam pecuniam mercator mihi pollicitus esset.**
    a. The judge was asking how much money the merchant promised me.
    b. The judge asked how much money the merchant had promised me.

79. **Cicero crimina exponit ut gravitatem causae intellegamus.**
    a. Cicero is explaining the charges so that we may understand the gravity of the case.
    b. Cicero explained the charges so that we might understand the gravity of the case.

80. **cum victimae sacrificatae essent, pontifex pauca verba dixit.**
    a. When the victims were being sacrificed, the priest said a few words.
    b. When the victims had been sacrificed, the priest said a few words.

XII Directions

Indicate the tense and voice of the underlined verbs.

    a. present active   c. pluperfect active
    b. imperfect active   d. pluperfect passive

81. amici tui <u>timebant</u> ne interfectus esses.

82. si diligentius laboravissem, dominus me <u>liberavisset</u>.

83. iudex rogavit quantam pecuniam mercator mihi <u>pollicitus esset</u>.

84. Cicero crimina <u>exponit</u> ut gravitatem causae intellegamus.

85. cum victimae <u>sacrificatae essent</u>, pontifex pauca verba dixit.

XIII Directions

Match the meaning to the English derivative.

86. vitiate   a. baseness, depravity

87. turpitude   b. formed by a compact

88. subsume   c. to spoil, corrupt; invalidate

89. federal   d. flagrant; remarkably bad

90. egregious   e. to include in a group; classify

****

91. profess   a. to set forth in detail

92. expound   b. boastfully vain and proud of oneself

93. rationale   c. fundamental reasons

94. vainglorious   d. disgusting; offensive

95. repulsive   e. to make an open declaration of; affirm

XIV Directions

Match the English derivative to its Latin root.

96. accommodate   a. repello

97. confess   b. progredior

98. enmity   c. inimicitia

99. progression   d. fateor

100. repellent   e. commodo

Stage 47 Test

PLEASE DO NOT WRITE ON THE TEST BOOKLET.
MARK ALL ANSWERS ON THE MACHINE SCORED ANSWER SHEET.

I Directions

Read the following passage.

After the "marriage" of Queen Dido and Aeneas, Rumor speeds through Libya stirring to anger all whom she meets. Eventually she provokes King Iarbus who prays to Jupiter complaining about the activities of Queen Dido and Aeneas. This passage contains Jupiter's response to King Iarbus' prayer.

talibus orantem dictis arasque tenentem	1
audiit **Omnipotens**, oculosque ad moenia **torsit**	2
regia et <u>oblitos</u> famae melioris <u>amantis</u>.	3
tum sic Mercurium adloquitur ac talia mandat:	4
"**vade** age, nate, voca **Zephyros** et **labere pinnis**	5
Dardaniumque ducem, Tyria Karthagine qui nunc	6
exspectat fatisque datas non **respicit** urbes,	7
adloquere et <u>celeris</u> **defer** mea dicta per <u>auras</u>."	8

Words and Phrases

Omnipotens - Almighty	**Zephyros: Zephyrus** - West Wind
torsit: torquere - turn	**labere: labi** - glide
regia: regius - royal	**pinnis: pinna** - wing
oblitos: oblivisci - forget	**respicit: respicere** - regard, consider
vade: vadere - go, make way	**defer: deferre** - carry down

II Directions

Select the correct answer based on the content and the grammar of the passage.

1. **In line 1 who is <u>orantem</u> and <u>tenentem</u>?**
   a. Jupiter   b. Mercury   c. Zephyr   d. King Iarbus

2. **In lines 2–3 to what does Jupiter turn his attention?**
   a. his eyes   c. the royal walls and forgetful lovers
   b. his walls   d. fame

3. **In lines 5–8 how many imperatives are there?**
   a. 4   b. 5   c. 6   d. 7

4. **In line 5 what two things does Jupiter suggest that Mercury use to aid his journey?**

    a. the Zephyrs and his own wings
    b. his age and his son
    c. shallow water and his lips

5. **In lines 6–8 what is Mercury's task?**

    a. to find Carthage and to look back over the cities
    b. to find Aeneas and to give him Jupiter's words
    c. to listen and to speak with swift words

III Directions

Match the definitions to their terms.

6.	*Aeneid*	a.	It deals with the war at Troy and the anger of Achilles.
7.	*Annales*	b.	It deals with the journey from Troy to the founding of Rome.
8.	*Iliad*	c.	It deals with the travels of a Greek leader as he sailed from Troy to Ithaca.
9.	in medias res	d.	It deals with the history of Rome from the flight from Troy until 181 B.C.
10.	*Odyssey*	e.	A starting point at the middle of the action

IV Directions

Indicate the correct answers to these questions about selections from the Stage 47 readings.

miratur molem Aeneas, magalia quondam,	1
miratur portas strepitumque et strata viarum.	2
instant ardentes Tyrii: pars ducere muros	3
molirique arcem et manibus subvolvere saxa,	4
pars optare locum tecto et concludere sulco;	5
iura magistratusque legunt sanctumque senatum.	6
hic portus alii effodiunt; hic alta theatris	7
fundamenta locant alii, immanisque columnas	8
rupibus excidunt, scaenis decora alta futuris.	9
"o fortunati, quorum iam moenia surgunt!"	10
Aeneas ait et fastigia suspicit urbis.	11

11. **In line 1 the poetic device is _____.**

    a. alliteration   b. assonance   c. apostrophe

12. **The scansion pattern of the first five feet of line 4 is _____.**
    a. D D S S D
    b. S S D D D
    c. S S D S D

13. **In line 5 the poetic device represented by <u>tecto</u> is _____.**
    a. alliteration   b. synecdoche   c. synchesis

14. **In line 6 the case of <u>iura, magistratus, sanctum,</u> and <u>senatum</u> is _____.**
    a. nominative   b. genitive   c. dative   d. accusative   e. ablative

15. **In line 8 the case of <u>immanis</u> is _____.**
    a. nominative   b. genitive   c. dative   d. accusative   e. ablative

16. **"o fortunati, quorum iam moenia surgunt!"**
    The poetic device represented by this line is _____.
    a. alliteration   b. assonance   c. apostrophe

****

uritur infelix Dido totaque vagatur	1
urbe furens, qualis coniecta cerva sagitta,	2
quam procul incautam nemora inter Cresia fixit	3
pastor agens telis liquitque volatile ferrum	4
nescius: illa fuga silvas saltusque peragrat	5
Dictaeos; haeret lateri letalis harundo.	6

17. **In line 1 the use of <u>uritur</u> indicates that Dido is _____.**
    a. literally on fire   b. consumed by hot passion   c. setting her city on fire

18. **In lines 2–6 Vergil compares _____.**
    a. Dido to an arrow and Aeneas to a deer
    b. Dido to a doe and Aeneas to the wood
    c. Dido to a doe and Aeneas to a hunter

19. **The poetic device displayed in lines 2–6 is a(n) _____.**
    a. metaphor   b. apostrophe   c. epic simile

20. **In line 6 the word order device represented is _____.**
    a. chiasmus   b. synchesis   c. parallel construction

21. **In line 6 the word that indicates foreshadowing is _____.**
    a. haeret   b. lateri   c. letalis   d. harundo

****

interea magno misceri murmure caelum   1
incipit, insequitur commixta grandine nimbus,   2
et Tyrii comites passim et Troiana iuventus   3
Dardaniusque nepos Veneris diversa per agros   4
tecta metu petiere; ruunt de montibus amnes.   5
speluncam Dido dux et Troianus eandem   6
deveniunt. prima et Tellus et pronuba Iuno   7
dant signum; fulsere ignes et conscius aether   8
conubiis, summoque ulularunt vertice Nymphae.   9
illa dies primus leti primusque malorum   10
causa fuit; neque enim specie famave movetur   11
nec iam furtivum Dido meditatur amorem: 12
coniugium vocat, hoc praetexit nomine culpam.   13

22. **In line 1 the poetic device represented is _____.**

    a. syncope   b. onomatopoeia   c. epic simile

23. **The action described in lines 1–2 indicates that _____.**

    a. a calm summer rain begins
    b. an active, violent storm begins
    c. the sky produces a winter scene complete with ice

24. **The action in lines 3–5 is highlighted by the use of _____.**

    a. spondees to indicate slow, solemn action
    b. dactyls to indicate frenetic activity as the storm approaches

25. **In line 5 <u>petiere</u> is an example of _____.**

    a. synecdoche   b. syncope   c. simile   d. synchesis

26. **In line 6 the word order device that highlights the action is _____.**

    a. chiasmus   b. framing   c. parallelism   d. synchesis

27. **In lines 7–9 indicate the number of deities and spirits who helped with the "wedding" ceremony.**

    a. 3   b. 4   c. 5

28. **In lines 11–13 Dido sees this episode as only one thing despite its appearance and rumor-causing effect. Indicate what Dido feels has happened.**

    a. a destructive storm   b. a harbinger of death   c. a wedding

29. **In line 13 Dido's use of <u>coniugium</u> in place of <u>culpam</u> is an example of _____.**

    a. allusion   b. connotation   c. euphemism

****

> "tu nunc Karthaginis altae   1
> fundamenta locas pulchramque uxorius urbem   2
> exstruis? heu, regni rerumque oblite tuarum!   3
> ipse deum tibi me claro demittit Olympo   4
> regnator, caelum ac terras qui numine torquet.   5
> ipse haec ferre iubet celeris mandata per auras: 6
> quid struis? aut qua spe Libycis teris otia terris?   7
> si te nulla movet tantarum gloria rerum,   8
> Ascanium surgentem et spes heredis Iuli   9
> respice, cui regnum Italiae Romanaque tellus debetur."   10

30. **In line 3 the case of words following <u>oblite</u> is _____.**
   a. nominative   b. genitive   c. dative   d. accusative   e. ablative

31. **In this entire passage the one tone of voice we might NOT imagine Mercury using is _____.**
   a. condescending   b. sympathetic   c. irritated   d. angry

32. **In line 6 the word order device used is _____.**
   a. chiasmus   b. framing   c. parallelism   d. synchesis

33. **In lines 8–11 Mercury suggests that if the "glory" of such a task does not move Aeneas, then he should at least think of his _____.**
   a. son   b. father   c. heirs

****

> "me patris Anchisae, quotiens umentibus umbris   1
> nox operit terras, quotiens astra ignea surgunt,   2
> admonet in somnis et turbida terret imago;   3
> me puer Ascanius capitisque iniuria cari,   4
> quem regno Hesperiae fraudo et fatalibus arvis.   5
> nunc etiam interpres divum Iove missus ab ipso   6
> (testor utrumque caput) celeris mandata per auras   7
> detulit: ipse deum manifesto in lumine vidi   8
> intrantem muros vocemque his auribus hausi.   9
> desine meque tuis incendere teque querelis;   10
> Italiam non sponte sequor."   11

34. **In lines 1–3 we learn that _____.**
   a. Aeneas bothers his father at night
   b. Anchises comes to Aeneas every night in dreams
   c. the stars and the lands are admonishing Aeneas

35. **In lines 4–5 we see that Aeneas feels he is _____.**
   a. cheating Ascanius out of his ordained lands
   b. injuring his son's head
   c. injuring the ordained fields

36. **In line 8 <u>ipse</u> modifies _____.**
   a. deum   b. manifesto   c. ego from vidi

37. **In lines 6–9 Aeneas explains that _____.**
   a. he has received orders from Jupiter himself
   b. he has received orders from an emissary of Jupiter
   c. he has been able to go through walls to hear the god's voice

38. **In line 10 the mood of <u>desine</u> is _____.**
   a. indicative   b. imperative   c. subjunctive

39. **In line 10 the case of <u>querelis</u> is _____.**
   a. nominative   b. genitive   c. dative   d. accusative   e. ablative

****

"haec precor, hanc vocem extremam cum sanguine fundo.	1
tum vos, o Tyrii, stirpem et genus omne futurum	2
exercete odiis, cinerique haec mittite nostro	3
munera. nullus amor populis nec foedera sunto.	4
exoriare aliquis nostris ex ossibus ultor	5
qui face Dardanios ferroque sequare colonos,	6
nunc, olim, quocumque dabunt se tempore vires,	7
litora litoribus contraria, fluctibus undas	8
imprecor, arma armis: pugnent ipsique nepotesque."	9

40. **In lines 1–4 Dido asks the Carthaginians to give her ashes as a gift. The gift is that they _____.**
   a. burn every Trojan in sight
   b. show love to the Trojans and enter into every treaty with them
   c. harass Aeneas' offspring and every future generation

41. **In lines 5–6 Dido prays that one of her offspring will play the role of _____.**
   a. avenger   b. colonist   c. sword maker

42. **In lines 7–9 Dido prays that her offspring and their offspring may fight on land and sea and _____.**
   a. boat-to-boat   b. hand-to-mouth   c. face-to-face

43. **Dido is predicting the coming of _____.**
   a. Julius Caesar   b. Mithridates   c. Hannibal

****

"dulces exuviae, dum fata deusque sinebat,   1
accipite hanc animam meque his exsolvite curis.   2
vixi et quem dederat cursum fortuna peregi,   3
et nunc magna mei sub terras ibit imago.   4
urbem praeclaram statui, mea moenia vidi,   5
ulta virum poenas inimico a fratre recepi,   6
felix, heu nimium felix, si litora tantum   7
numquam Dardaniae tetigissent nostra carinae."   8

dixit, et os impressa toro "moriemur inultae,   9
sed moriamur" ait. "sic, sic iuvat ire sub umbras.   10
hauriat hunc oculis ignem crudelis ab alto   11
Dardanus, et nostrae secum ferat omina mortis."   12

44. **In lines 1–2 Dido asks that _____ .**

   a. the gods forbid her action
   b. her spirit be received and that she is set free from cares
   c. her spirit set him free from his cares

45. **In line 3 we sense that Dido _____ .**

   a. is tired
   b. has cursed her fortune
   c. feels she has lived her allotted amount of time

46. **In lines 5–6 Dido relates that she has _____ .**

   a. accomplished three great acts
   b. accomplished two great acts
   c. not accomplished what she had wanted

47. **In line 8 <u>carinae</u> is an example of _____ .**

   a. synchesis   b. syncope   c. synecdoche

48. **In line 9 <u>moriemur</u> represents a(n) _____ .**

   a. statement of fact   b. command   c. exhortation

49. **In line 10 <u>moriamur</u> represents a(n) _____ .**

   a. statement of fact   b. command   c. exhortation

50. **Lines 11–12 contain Dido's last _____ .**

   a. prayer   b. curse on Aeneas   c. loving thoughts

V Directions

Indicate the type of epic the following characteristics describe.

a. Homeric   b. Vergilian   c. common to both

51. It is a long narrative poem related in an elevated style.

52. Its narrative was meant to be sung in camps and at public gatherings.

53. It centered around a hero of national, historical, or legendary significance.

54. It dealt with the Greek warrior Achilles.

55. It dealt with the Trojan survivor Aeneas and his people.

56. This is a literary piece written by a sophisticated craftsman.

57. It dealt with Odysseus' travels to home.

58. Its setting was vast in scope covering many nations.

59. Its action consists of battles or journeys that require courage or heroic deeds.

60. Gods, goddesses, and other supernatural forces take an interest in the action as well as intervene from time to time.

VI Directions

*Indicate whether the following culture statements are true or false by marking **a** for **true** and **b** for **false**.*

61. Most epics began with an invocation to a Muse to help with the writing.

62. The action always starts slowly at the beginning of the storyline and progresses methodically through the narrative.

63. Flashbacks are used to fill in exposition of earlier events.

64. There are extended formal speeches by main characters.

65. There are epic similes that are short comparisons which deal only with the specific point of parallel.

VII Directions

Match the Latin word to its synonym.

66.	comparare	a.	hortari
67.	discedere	b.	proficisci
68.	incitare	c.	polliceri
69.	promittere	d.	regredi
70.	revenire	e.	adipisci

****

71.	amnis	a.	mortuus
72.	astra	b.	imber
73.	letalis	c.	relinquo
74.	linquo	d.	flumen
75.	nimbus	e.	sidera

****

76.	Cresia	a.	Trojan
77.	Dardanius	b.	Carthaginian
78.	Hesperia	c.	silva
79.	nemus	d.	Western Land
80.	Tyrius	e.	Cretan

VIII Directions

Match the meaning to the English derivative.

81.	extravagant	a.	an established law
82.	statute	b.	favoritism shown to relatives
83.	passim	c.	excessive; wasteful
84.	nepotism	d.	to renounce; recant
85.	abjure	e.	throughout

****

86. vagabond   a. to set forth in detail

87. specify   b. accompanying; concomitant

88. ossify   c. to settle or fix rigidly

89. collateral   d. to be continually changing

90. fluctuate   e. wandering; shiftless

IX   Directions

Match the correct definition to the character it describes.

91. Aeneas   a. father of Aeneas

92. Anchises   b. city in northern Africa

93. Ascanius   c. son of Aeneas

94. Carthage   d. a native of Tyre

95. Dido   e. son of Venus

X   Directions

Match the author to the names of his work(s).

96. Greek *Iliad*   a. Ennius

97. Greek *Odyssey*   b. Homer

98. Roman *Odyssey*   c. Livius Andronicus

99. *Annales*   d. Vergil

100. *Aeneid*

Stage 48 Test

PLEASE DO NOT WRITE ON THE TEST BOOKLET.
MARK ALL ANSWERS ON THE MACHINE SCORED ANSWER SHEET.

I Directions

Read the following passage.

iam res Romana adeo erat valida, ut **cuilibet finitimarum civitatum**	1
bello par esset; sed **penuria** mulierum hominis aetatem **duratura**	2
magnitudo erat, **quippe** quibus nec domi spes **prolis** nec cum finitimis	3
conubia essent. tum ex consilio patrum Romulus legatos **circa** vicinas	4
gentes misit, qui **societatem** conubiumque novo populo peterent.	5

Words and Phrases

cuilibet: quilibet - anyone
finitimarum: finitimus - neighboring
civitatum: civitas - state
penuria: penuria - need
duratura: durare - endure, last

quippe - since
prolis: proles - offspring
conubia: conubium - right to intermarry
circa - around
societatem: societas - alliance

II Directions

Select the correct answer based on the content and the grammar of the passage.

1. **In lines 1–2 we learn that the Roman state was so strong that it was _____.**
   a. part of the war with neighboring states
   b. equal in war to any neighboring state
   c. as beautiful as any neighboring state

2. **In line 2 the use of <u>esset</u> is _____.**
   a. indirect command   b. purpose clause   c. result clause

3. **In line 2 we learn that the greatness of the new Roman state would last _____.**
   a. for one generation   b. forever   c. for a few summers

4. **In line 2 we learn that the problem for the new Roman state was a _____.**
   a. lack of horses   b. lack of men   c. lack of women

5. **In line 2 <u>duratura</u> is a _____ participle.**
   a. present active   b. perfect passive   c. future active

6. **In lines 3–4 we learn that the Romans had no _____ with their neighbors.**
   a. alliances   b. marriage rights   c. relatives

7. **In line 3 the case of <u>domi</u> is _____.**
   a. dative   b. genitive   c. locative   d. accusative   e. ablative

8. **In line 4 we learn that Romulus received advice from _____.**
   a. his senate   b. his envoys   c. his neighbors

9. **In lines 4–5 we learn that the one thing Romulus did NOT ask for from his neighbors was _____.**
   a. alliance   b. rights of marriage   c. new people

10. **In line 5 the use of <u>peterent</u> is _____.**
    a. indirect command   b. purpose clause   c. result clause

III Directions

Match the name of the person to his/her Latin description.

    a. Amulius   b. Faustulus   c. Mars   d. Rea Silva   e. she-wolf

11. vi compressa Vestalis cum geminum partum edidisset

12. pulso fratre **** regnat. addit sceleri scelus: stirpem fratris virilem interemit, fratris filiae Reae Silviae per speciem honoris, cum Vestalem eam legisset, perpetua virginitate spem partus adimit.

13. **** sitientem ex montibus qui circa sunt ad puerilem vagitum cursum flexisse; eam submissas infantibus adeo mitem praebuisse mammas ut lingua lambentem pueros

14. quia deus auctor culpae honestior erat, **** incertae stirpis patrem nuncupat.

15. pueros magister regii pecoris invenerit.

****

    a. Larentia   b. Remus   c. Romulus   d. Romulus et Remus   e. Tiber

16. forte quadam divinitus super ripas **** effusus lenibus stagnis et posse quamvis languida mergi aqua infantes spem ferentibus dabat.

17. ab eo ad stabula **** uxori educandos datos. sunt qui **** vulgato corpore "lupam" inter pastores vocatam putent.

18. ita Numitori Albana re permissa **** cupido cepit in iis locis ubi expositi ubique educati erant urbis condendae.

19. iamque nuntiato augurio cum duplex numerus **** se ostendisset.

20. priori **** augurium venisse fertur, sex vultures.

IV   Directions

Indicate the use of the <u>underlined</u> grammar points.

21. <u>**pulso fratre**</u> ****** regnat.**
    a. ablative of agent   b. ablative absolute   c. ablative of means

22. **Faustulo <u>fuisse</u> nomen ferunt.**

    <u>**fuisse**</u> is a _____ infinitive.
    a. present active   b. present passive   c. perfect active   d. perfect passive

23. **ita <u>geniti</u> itaque educati, cum primum adolevit aetas, nec in stabulis nec ad pecora segnes venando peragrare saltus.**

    <u>**geniti**</u> is a _____ participle.
    a. present active   b. perfect active   c. perfect passive

24. **ita geniti itaque educati, cum primum adolevit aetas, nec in stabulis nec ad pecora segnes <u>venando</u> peragrare saltus.**

    <u>**venando**</u> is used as a _____.
    a. gerund – noun   b. gerundive – purpose   c. gerundive – adjective

25. **ita geniti itaque educati, cum primum adolevit aetas, nec in stabulis nec ad pecora segnes venando <u>peragrare</u> saltus.**

    <u>**peragrare**</u> is an example of _____.
    a. complementary infinitive   b. historical infinitive   c. syncope

26. **et <u>supererat</u> multitudo Albanorum Latinorumque.**

    The tense of <u>**supererat**</u> is_____.
    a. present   b. imperfect   c. perfect   d. pluperfect

27. **ad id pastores quoque <u>accesserant</u>.**

    The tense of <u>**accesserant**</u> is _____.
    a. present   b. imperfect   c. perfect   d. pluperfect

28. **Palatium Romulus, Remus Aventinum ad <u>inaugurandum</u> capiunt.**

    The use of <u>**inaugurandum**</u> is _____.
    a. gerund – noun   b. gerund – purpose   c. gerundive – adjective

29. **hi numero <u>avium</u> regnum trahebantur.**

    The case of <u>**avium**</u> is _____.
    a. nominative   b. genitive   c. dative   d. accusative   e. ablative

30. **ita solus potitus <u>imperio</u> Romulus.**

    The case of <u>**imperio**</u> is _____.
    a. nominative   b. genitive   c. dative   d. accusative   e. ablative

V Directions

Select the correct answers to complete these culture statements.

31. **Livy was writing about events that took place _____ years before he lived.**
    a. 600   b. 700   c. 800

32. **The events were probably more _____ than history.**
    a. legends   b. facts   c. impressions

33. **Due to this fact, it is no wonder that Livy included _____.**
    a. only one version of the events he described
    b. several versions of the events he described

34. **When dealing with history, Livy states that it is only the _____ of what has been done.**
    a. expressions   b. deeds   c. memory

35. **History provides readers with exempla. Select the one item to which exempla do NOT pertain.**
    a. patterns of conduct for individuals to imitate or to avoid
    b. patterns of conduct for states to imitate or to avoid
    c. selections of religious tenets

36. **The major focus of the three historians mentioned in the culture readings seems to be on _____.**
    a. facts   b. people   c. events

VI Directions

Select the correct Latin sentence for the English translation.

37. **I was afraid that the soldiers would catch me.**
    a. timebam ne milites me caperent.
    b. timebam ne a militibus caperer.

38. **You must hide in the forest so that you will not be seen by the enemies.**
    a. in silva tibi latendum est ne hostes te videant.
    b. in silva tibi latendum est ne ab hostibus videaris.

39. **The master wants to find out whether the slaves are preparing dinner.**
    a. dominus cognoscere vult num servi cenam parent.
    b. dominus cognoscere vult num cena a servis paretur.

40. **Tell me why the slaves are never praised by their master.**
    a. dic mihi quare dominus numquam servos laudet.
    b. dic mihi quare servi numquam a domino laudentur.

VII Directions

Match the meaning to the English derivative.

41. intervene   a. to think, suppose

42. opine   b. justification

43. ratify   c. to come between

44. vindication   d. to approve, confirm

45. reflexive   e. a verb whose subject and direct object are identical

****

46. divulge   a. to cause to vanish

47. dispel   b. twelve

48. inflexible   c. stiff, rigid

49. dozen   d. means of support or livelihood

50. subsistence   e. to make known; reveal

VIII Directions

Match the grammar term to its definition.

    a. historical infinitive   b. historical present   c. syncope

51. _____ is used to describe events happening in the past and occurs most often in descriptions of lively and rapid action. It is always the second principal part.

52. _____ is used for an event which has obviously happened in the past and is used to make the narrative more lively and vivid as if the action were happening before the reader's eyes. This is always written with a personal ending.

53. _____ is used to make a verb fit the metric pattern of a line of poetry. It can also be found in prose. It looks like an infinitive but is not.

IX Directions

Match the name of the grammar term to the sentences below.

a. historical infinitive   b. historical present   c. syncope

54. fur per fenestram intravit. omnia tacita erant; subito sonitum **audit**.

55. mater **orare hortari iubere** ut fugerem.

56. servi contra dominum **coniuravere**.

57. omnes amici **bibere cantare saltare**.

58. dum feles **abit**, mures luserunt.

X Directions

Match the name of the author to his work(s).

59. *Lives of the Twelve Caesars*   a. Livy

60. *Annales*   b. Suetonius

61. *Ab Urbe Condita Libri*   c. Tacitus

62. *Agricola*

XI Directions

Select the correct tense/voice designation for the given subjunctive verbs.

63. **caperet**
    a. present passive   c. perfect passive
    b. imperfect active   d. pluperfect active

64. **captus sit**
    a. present passive   c. perfect passive
    b. imperfect active   d. pluperfect active

65. **cepisset**
    a. present passive   c. perfect passive
    b. imperfect active   d. pluperfect active

66. **capiatur**
    a. present passive   c. perfect passive
    b. imperfect active   d. pluperfect active

67. **captus esset**

    a. present active   c. perfect active

    b. imperfect passive   d. pluperfect passive

68. **caperetur**

    a. present active   c. perfect active

    b. imperfect passive   d. pluperfect passive

69. **capiat**

    a. present active   c. perfect active

    b. imperfect passive   d. pluperfect passive

70. **ceperit**

    a. present active   c. perfect active

    b. imperfect passive   d. pluperfect passive

XII Directions

Indicate the type of subjunctive found in the following examples.

    a. adverbial purpose   c. positive purpose   e. result

    b. negative purpose   d. relative purpose

71. imperator milites misit qui signum amissum invenirent.

72. canis in speluncam cucurrit quo celaret.

73. rex captivis liberavit ne crudelis videretur.

74. tantus est strepitus ut omnes terreamur.

75. puer stetit ut pompam videret.

****

    a. causal   c. hortatory   e. verb of fearing

    b. concessive   d. jussive

76. Salvius nunc respondeat.

77. proficiscamur.

78. cum me rideret, iratus non fiebam.

79. amici tui timebant ne interfectus esses.

80. cum me rideret, iratus fiebam.

a. result   d. indirect deliberative question

b. deliberative question   e. indirect question

c. indirect command

81. dicite mihi quot hostes capti sint.

82. pueri tam celeriter fugerunt ut a custodibus non caperentur.

83. miles me monuit ne ad aedificium starem.

84. quo eam?

85. milites incerti erant utrum cederent an resisterent.

XIII Directions

Match the definitions to the names.

86. Aeneas   a. Aeneas' wife

87. Alba Longa   b. town founded by Aeneas

88. Ascanius   c. town founded by Aeneas' son

89. Lavinia   d. established a new home in Italy for the Trojans

90. Lavinium   e. son of Aeneas

****

91. Amulius   a. rightful ruler of Alba Longa after Proca

92. Mars   b. power-hungry son of Proca

93. Numitor   c. daughter of Numitor

94. Proca   d. purported father of the twins

95. Rea Silva   e. man who was king of Alba Longa and who had two sons

****

96. Faustulus   a. twin brother who saw six vultures and was later murdered

97. Larentia

     b. where the twins were exposed to the elements

98. Romulus

     c. shepherd who found the twins

99. Remus   d. wife of the shepherd; she took care of the twins

100. Ruminal fig-tree   e. twin brother who saw 12 vultures

Answers to the Stage Tests

Unit 4 – Stage 35 Test Key

1. e	26. c	51. c	76. d
2. c	27. b	52. a	77. d
3. c	28. a	53. b	78. c
4. a	29. d	54. e	79. d
5. a	30. c	55. d	80. a
6. c	31. b	56. a	81. a
7. a	32. a	57. c	82. b
8. c	33. d	58. b	83. a
9. b	34. c	59. b	84. b
10. d	35. a	60. c	85. a
11. c	36. a	61. b	86. c
12. a	37. e	62. b	87. e
13. c	38. d	63. a	88. d
14. b	39. b	64. c	89. b
15. b	40. c	65. b	90. a
16. b	41. e	66. c	91. b
17. a	42. c	67. a	92. a
18. c	43. d	68. e	93. a
19. a	44. a	69. b	94. b
20. c	45. b	70. d	95. a
21. d	46. c	71. c	96. b
22. c	47. e	72. d	97. b
23. d	48. a	73. e	98. b
24. a	49. b	74. a	99. a
25. d	50. d	75. b	100. b

Unit 4 – Stage 36 Test Key

1. b	26. c	51. d	76. a
2. c	27. b	52. b	77. c
3. b	28. b	53. c	78. c
4. a	29. c	54. a	79. a
5. c	30. c	55. b	80. c
6. a	31. e	56. b	81. e
7. c	32. a	57. d	82. c
8. c	33. c	58. a	83. d
9. b	34. d	59. e	84. b
10. b	35. b	60. c	85. a
11. b	36. b	61. b	86. d
12. a	37. b	62. a	87. c
13. a	38. a	63. c	88. e
14. a	39. d	64. c	89. a
15. b	40. a	65. d	90. b
16. a	41. a	66. d	91. b
17. a	42. b	67. b	92. a
18. c	43. d	68. c	93. a
19. b	44. a	69. d	94. b
20. a	45. c	70. c	95. a
21. c	46. b	71. b	96. b
22. c	47. d	72. a	97. a
23. a	48. a	73. c	98. b
24. d	49. c	74. d	99. b
25. b	50. b	75. d	100. a

Unit 4 – Stage 37 Test Key

1. b	26. c	51. c	76. b
2. c	27. a	52. b	77. d
3. b	28. b	53. e	78. a
4. a	29. d	54. a	79. e
5. a	30. c	55. b	80. c
6. c	31. b	56. d	81. b
7. b	32. c	57. e	82. c
8. a	33. a	58. c	83. a
9. b	34. b	59. a	84. a
10. b	35. a	60. b	85. d
11. a	36. a	61. b	86. b
12. a	37. b	62. b	87. c
13. a	38. c	63. b	88. a
14. a	39. c	64. b	89. e
15. b	40. c	65. b	90. d
16. a	41. b	66. a	91. e
17. a	42. a	67. a	92. c
18. b	43. b	68. a	93. d
19. c	44. a	69. a	94. b
20. a	45. a	70. b	95. a
21. b	46. b	71. b	96. d
22. a	47. b	72. e	97. e
23. b	48. d	73. d	98. a
24. b	49. e	74. a	99. b
25. a	50. b	75. c	100. c

Unit 4 – Stage 38 Test Key

1. c	26. c	51. d	76. d
2. b	27. b	52. e	77. b
3. b	28. c	53. c	78. e
4. a	29. a	54. a	79. a
5. c	30. a	55. b	80. c
6. b	31. c	56. c	81. d
7. c	32. a	57. e	82. c
8. a	33. c	58. d	83. b
9. b	34. b	59. a	84. e
10. b	35. a	60. b	85. a
11. b	36. b	61. b	86. d
12. a	37. a	62. d	87. c
13. a	38. c	63. b	88. e
14. c	39. c	64. a	89. b
15. a	40. b	65. b	90. a
16. c	41. b	66. d	91. d
17. a	42. a	67. c	92. c
18. e	43. b	68. a	93. a
19. c	44. a	69. b	94. b
20. c	45. a	70. d	95. e
21. c	46. b	71. b	96. c
22. a	47. a	72. c	97. e
23. c	48. b	73. c	98. a
24. c	49. a	74. b	99. b
25. c	50. a	75. a	100. d

Unit 4 – Stage 39 Test Key

1. b	26. b	51. b	76. b
2. c	27. c	52. c	77. a
3. a	28. b	53. b	78. a
4. c	29. a	54. a	79. a
5. a	30. a	55. b	80. a
6. c	31. c	56. b	81. b
7. b	32. c	57. d	82. b
8. c	33. d	58. d	83. b
9. c	34. c	59. b	84. b
10. b	35. a	60. b	85. b
11. a	36. c	61. d	86. b
12. c	37. b	62. a	87. b
13. a	38. a	63. c	88. a
14. b	39. b	64. b	89. b
15. b	40. a	65. d	90. a
16. c	41. c	66. b	91. e
17. a	42. e	67. a	92. a
18. e	43. a	68. b	93. b
19. b	44. b	69. a	94. d
20. c	45. d	70. a	95. c
21. b	46. e	71. a	96. e
22. a	47. a	72. d	97. d
23. b	48. d	73. e	98. b
24. b	49. c	74. b	99. c
25. b	50. b	75. c	100. a

Unit 4 – Stage 40 Test Key

1. c	26. b	51. b	76. b
2. d	27. c	52. a	77. c
3. b	28. a	53. b	78. d
4. a	29. e	54. b	79. e
5. c	30. d	55. a	80. a
6. b	31. d	56. b	81. c
7. b	32. a	57. e	82. d
8. a	33. e	58. d	83. e
9. d	34. b	59. c	84. b
10. c	35. c	60. a	85. a
11. c	36. c	61. e	86. d
12. b	37. a	62. d	87. a
13. b	38. d	63. a	88. e
14. c	39. b	64. c	89. c
15. a	40. a	65. b	90. b
16. b	41. b	66. e	91. c
17. a	42. a	67. d	92. e
18. a	43. b	68. a	93. d
19. c	44. a	69. c	94. b
20. a	45. d	70. b	95. a
21. c	46. c	71. b	96. d
22. c	47. a	72. a	97. e
23. b	48. b	73. a	98. a
24. a	49. c	74. b	99. c
25. c	50. b	75. a	100. b

Unit 4 – Stage 41 Test Key

1. b	26. b	51. e	76. b
2. c	27. d	52. a	77. a
3. c	28. a	53. d	78. c
4. a	29. b	54. c	79. c
5. c	30. c	55. b	80. b
6. b	31. a	56. d	81. a
7. b	32. b	57. b	82. b
8. a	33. a	58. a	83. b
9. b	34. c	59. b	84. a
10. c	35. a	60. c	85. b
11. b	36. a	61. b	86. a
12. d	37. a	62. a	87. b
13. a	38. b	63. b	88. a
14. e	39. b	64. a	89. a
15. c	40. a	65. a	90. b
16. a	41. b	66. b	91. d
17. c	42. a	67. b	92. a
18. b	43. b	68. a	93. e
19. b	44. a	69. b	94. c
20. a	45. b	70. a	95. b
21. b	46. d	71. a	96. c
22. b	47. a	72. a	97. a
23. a	48. e	73. a	98. b
24. b	49. b	74. b	99. e
25. c	50. c	75. a	100. d

Unit 4 – Stage 42 Test Key

1. a	26. c	51. a	76. b
2. a	27. b	52. b	77. d
3. c	28. a	53. a	78. a
4. b	29. d	54. c	79. c
5. e	30. a	55. a	80. e
6. d	31. d	56. a	81. a
7. a	32. c	57. b	82. b
8. c	33. d	58. b	83. a
9. c	34. a	59. c	84. a
10. c	35. e	60. c	85. c
11. b	36. b	61. e	86. b
12. d	37. b	62. d	87. c
13. a	38. d	63. b	88. a
14. a	39. a	64. a	89. b
15. b	40. c	65. c	90. a
16. d	41. a	66. b	91. b
17. a	42. b	67. e	92. a
18. d	43. a	68. d	93. e
19. a	44. c	69. c	94. d
20. d	45. b	70. a	95. c
21. c	46. a	71. b	96. c
22. c	47. a	72. e	97. a
23. b	48. a	73. d	98. e
24. c	49. a	74. a	99. d
25. e	50. a	75. c	100. b

Unit 4 – Stage 43 Test Key

1. b	26. a	51. a	76. b
2. a	27. a	52. c	77. a
3. b	28. a	53. b	78. c
4. d	29. b	54. d	79. b
5. b	30. a	55. b	80. c
6. c	31. b	56. a	81. a
7. a	32. a	57. e	82. a
8. d	33. b	58. c	83. a
9. a	34. a	59. b	84. c
10. c	35. b	60. c	85. b
11. c	36. d	61. a	86. c
12. b	37. b	62. a	87. e
13. a	38. d	63. b	88. b
14. a	39. a	64. b	89. a
15. b	40. c	65. a	90. d
16. e	41. d	66. b	91. d
17. d	42. b	67. a	92. a
18. a	43. d	68. b	93. e
19. b	44. b	69. c	94. b
20. c	45. b	70. d	95. c
21. b	46. e	71. b	96. c
22. b	47. d	72. d	97. a
23. b	48. b	73. c	98. d
24. a	49. a	74. d	99. e
25. b	50. c	75. d	100. b

Unit 4 – Stage 44 Test Key

1. b	26. c	51. b	76. c
2. d	27. e	52. a	77. b
3. b	28. d	53. a	78. c
4. c	29. a	54. c	79. a
5. b	30. b	55. a	80. b
6. c	31. c	56. b	81. c
7. a	32. d	57. a	82. d
8. c	33. b	58. b	83. b
9. c	34. e	59. a	84. d
10. b	35. a	60. b	85. a
11. c	36. e	61. a	86. e
12. e	37. a	62. c	87. d
13. d	38. c	63. d	88. b
14. a	39. b	64. d	89. a
15. b	40. d	65. c	90. c
16. c	41. e	66. a	91. b
17. a	42. b	67. b	92. d
18. e	43. d	68. b	93. a
19. b	44. c	69. a	94. e
20. d	45. a	70. b	95. c
21. d	46. a	71. d	96. c
22. c	47. a	72. b	97. d
23. b	48. c	73. a	98. e
24. e	49. b	74. c	99. a
25. a	50. d	75. a	100. b

Unit 4 – Stage 45 Test Key

1. c	26. a	51. b	76. b
2. a	27. c	52. a	77. e
3. b	28. b	53. c	78. d
4. b	29. d	54. b	79. c
5. a	30. a	55. d	80. a
6. a	31. b	56. b	81. b
7. c	32. c	57. c	82. a
8. b	33. d	58. b	83. a
9. a	34. a	59. d	84. b
10. e	35. c	60. a	85. b
11. b	36. e	61. c	86. c
12. a	37. d	62. b	87. d
13. b	38. a	63. a	88. b
14. a	39. c	64. d	89. e
15. b	40. b	65. c	90. a
16. c	41. d	66. c	91. c
17. a	42. b	67. d	92. e
18. b	43. e	68. e	93. a
19. b	44. c	69. a	94. b
20. a	45. a	70. b	95. d
21. d	46. b	71. c	96. a
22. c	47. a	72. d	97. e
23. b	48. b	73. a	98. b
24. b	49. b	74. b	99. c
25. d	50. a	75. e	100. d

Unit 4 – Stage 46 Test Key

1. b	26. e	51. b	76. b
2. c	27. c	52. b	77. a
3. a	28. a	53. e	78. b
4. b	29. d	54. a	79. a
5. c	30. b	55. b	80. b
6. b	31. b	56. a	81. b
7. c	32. e	57. a	82. c
8. d	33. d	58. b	83. d
9. a	34. a	59. b	84. a
10. c	35. c	60. a	85. d
11. d	36. b	61. d	86. c
12. c	37. d	62. a	87. a
13. b	38. a	63. e	88. e
14. a	39. c	64. c	89. b
15. c	40. e	65. b	90. d
16. c	41. b	66. c	91. e
17. a	42. a	67. e	92. a
18. d	43. c	68. a	93. c
19. a	44. e	69. d	94. b
20. a	45. d	70. b	95. d
21. c	46. c	71. b	96. e
22. c	47. e	72. a	97. d
23. d	48. c	73. d	98. c
24. b	49. b	74. e	99. b
25. c	50. a	75. c	100. a

Unit 4 – Stage 47 Test Key

1. d	26. b	51. c	76. e
2. c	27. b	52. a	77. a
3. c	28. c	53. c	78. d
4. a	29. c	54. a	79. c
5. b	30. b	55. b	80. b
6. b	31. b	56. b	81. c
7. d	32. d	57. a	82. a
8. a	33. a	58. c	83. e
9. e	34. b	59. c	84. b
10. c	35. a	60. c	85. d
11. a	36. c	61. a	86. e
12. c	37. b	62. b	87. a
13. b	38. b	63. a	88. c
14. d	39. e	64. a	89. b
15. d	40. c	65. b	90. d
16. c	41. a	66. e	91. e
17. b	42. c	67. b	92. a
18. c	43. c	68. a	93. c
19. c	44. b	69. c	94. b
20. a	45. c	70. d	95. d
21. c	46. b	71. d	96. b
22. b	47. c	72. e	97. b
23. b	48. a	73. a	98. c
24. b	49. c	74. c	99. a
25. b	50. b	75. b	100. d

Unit 4 – Stage 48 Test Key

1. b	26. b	51. a	76. d
2. c	27. d	52. b	77. c
3. a	28. b	53. c	78. b
4. c	29. b	54. b	79. e
5. c	30. e	55. a	80. a
6. b	31. b	56. c	81. e
7. c	32. a	57. a	82. a
8. a	33. b	58. b	83. c
9. c	34. c	59. b	84. b
10. b	35. c	60. c	85. d
11. d	36. b	61. a	86. d
12. a	37. a	62. c	87. c
13. e	38. b	63. b	88. e
14. c	39. a	64. c	89. a
15. b	40. b	65. d	90. b
16. e	41. c	66. a	91. b
17. a	42. a	67. d	92. d
18. d	43. d	68. b	93. a
19. c	44. b	69. a	94. e
20. b	45. e	70. c	95. c
21. b	46. e	71. d	96. c
22. c	47. a	72. a	97. d
23. c	48. c	73. b	98. e
24. a	49. b	74. e	99. a
25. b	50. d	75. c	100. b

STUDENT ANSWER SHEET

Test for Stage _____   **Name:**_____

1. ___	26. ___	51. ___	76. ___
2. ___	27. ___	52. ___	77. ___
3. ___	28. ___	53. ___	78. ___
4. ___	29. ___	54. ___	79. ___
5. ___	30. ___	55. ___	80. ___
6. ___	31. ___	56. ___	81. ___
7. ___	32. ___	57. ___	82. ___
8. ___	33. ___	58. ___	83. ___
9. ___	34. ___	59. ___	84. ___
10. ___	35. ___	60. ___	85. ___
11. ___	36. ___	61. ___	86. ___
12. ___	37. ___	62. ___	87. ___
13. ___	38. ___	63. ___	88. ___
14. ___	39. ___	64. ___	89. ___
15. ___	40. ___	65. ___	90. ___
16. ___	41. ___	66. ___	91. ___
17. ___	42. ___	67. ___	92. ___
18. ___	43. ___	68. ___	93. ___
19. ___	44. ___	69. ___	94. ___
20. ___	45. ___	70. ___	95. ___
21. ___	46. ___	71. ___	96. ___
22. ___	47. ___	72. ___	97. ___
23. ___	48. ___	73. ___	98. ___
24. ___	49. ___	74. ___	99. ___
25. ___	50. ___	75. ___	100. ___